# RELAPSE

*To my father, Keith, who never got to see his son become the boy he could be proud of. I miss you so very much. To my mother, Donna, who has always shown me support and tremendous love. To my best friend, Casey, who always made me feel human when I felt like a monster. And to my wonderful wife, Jenna, who has been with me through the toughest times in my life. I love you.*

# Contents

# Proud Alcoholic

I was a proud alcoholic. All of the best fishermen were alcoholics and I wanted to be just like them. But before long my addiction overpowered me. I became an alcoholic, an addict, and a criminal. I became the man I most feared. Guilt stricken and ashamed, I thought I was doomed to death. In fact, I never thought I'd survive past the age of twenty-five. But before my addiction, and long before I was a fisherman, I was just a skateboarder.

———•—

Skateboarding was my first addiction. It was my original drug. Growing up in the small town of Anacortes, Washington, in the '90s, skateboarding wasn't popular. You weren't *supposed* to skate. But from the time my cousin, Josh Petrin, brought me with him to buy his first skateboard when I was ten years old, skateboarding was my life. Josh was seven years older than me and someone that I looked up to. I saw him and his cousin, Jason, living the skateboarding lifestyle and I wanted to be just like them. When they told me what some of the most talented guys could make their skateboards do, like flipping their boards or making their boards jump to their knees, I knew that I wanted to do that, too.

By the time I was thirteen, I was meeting my friends every day after school behind the Safeway store in Anacortes to skate. We'd all dress up to try to *be* skateboarders. We'd put on oversized shorts, beanies, and mustard colored sweatshirts, and we'd skate till dark. I loved skateboarding, but I didn't fit in. In fact, I was horrible at it. I could barely stay on my board and I was terrified of falling. But every day I watched my friends skate and I tried to copy what I saw. Slowly I started picking it up—but it didn't come easy. It took me over a year to learn how to kick flip and after that I was too scared to jump even three

stairs. It took me a while to catch on, but after another year of practicing I finally started to improve. I began skateboarding all the time, and the more I practiced, the better I got.

In Anacortes, kids like me didn't exist. I was a skateboarder living in a small town where skating was taboo. There were no skateboarding competitions. There were no skateparks. There was no way for me to see if I had any real talent. All that I had were some skateboarding magazines and a few professional demos to watch. Those were the only times that I could see what professional skateboarders *actually* did. I had no idea that the tricks I saw in those magazines were the *best tricks* the pros could do. I was able to imitate a lot of what I saw, and I didn't realize that was anything out of the ordinary. I was just doing what came natural. By the time I was seventeen, I started doing tremendously well for myself. As my addiction to the sport grew, I wanted to see how good I could get and how far skateboarding could take me.

When I was a senior at Anacortes High School, I partnered up with my best friend, Casey Rigney, and we started skating together every day. We fed off each other and we became inseparable. Whatever we did, we were always together. Kids at my school used to tease Casey. He had bright red hair and looked kind of nerdy, so they would call him *red* or *nerd*. But I stood up for him. He was my best friend and the only person I knew who could outskate me. Casey was more of a technical skater. He could do almost every trick left-handed and right-handed. He did a lot of manuals, ledges, and handrails. He was known for the way that he could make his board slide and grind on long handrails. He could do anything he wanted with a skateboard. I had a lot fewer tricks, but I was notorious for jumping huge stairs by the time I was eighteen. I used to practice by jumping off ten foot tall shipping containers that were lined up behind the Safeway store. I would climb on top of the containers, run full sprint, jump on my board, and do tricks off them to practice.

The more Casey and I skated, the more we believed that we were destined to become pro skateboarders. I already knew that I wasn't going to college. I didn't have the grades and skateboarding was all that I cared about. We wondered what it would take to find sponsors who would actually pay us to skate. When you're eighteen and living in a small town like Anacortes, getting paid to skateboard would mean you're God. We knew that if we wanted to make it as professionals, we'd have to start producing skate videos that demoed our tricks. Filming at the Safeway in Anacortes wouldn't help us at all. It was an unknown spot in a small town that no one cared about. We wanted to find a popular skating spot that sponsors would pay attention to. The closest place to Anacortes that had any kind of skateboarding crowd was Vancouver. The drive from Anacortes to Vancouver was only about two hours, and it was before 9/11, so it was still easy to cross the Canadian border. Casey and I would just grab our IDs, get in his car, and head up north.

We ended up going to Vancouver almost every weekend when I was eighteen, and those were some of the best times of my life. Vancouver was the first place we had ever been to where there were other guys like us. In Anacortes we were outcasts, but in Vancouver we found other skateboarders trying to push the sport like we were. The skateparks in Vancouver were well known to sponsors, too. They knew the terrain, how big the stairs were, and how long the rails were at places like White Rock Skatepark and Griffin Skatepark. That meant the footage we shot there would actually mean something. We had no idea what sponsors were looking for, so we would leaf through our skateboarding magazines like *Transworld* and *Big Brother*, pick out the Vancouver skate spots, and then go to those locations and film ourselves doing tricks that had never been tried there. We thought that if the sponsors liked what they saw, then we were in. Looking back now, it wasn't a bad idea, but Casey and I were definitely a different brood. Most amateurs were skating in competitions to find sponsors, but we were doing it our own way.

On the way home from one of our Vancouver trips, Casey and I decided that I needed to go where the best skateboarding connections were if we were serious about turning pro. Vancouver was definitely an improvement over Anacortes, but the best skateboarding at the time was down south in

Los Angeles and San Diego. I don't remember whose idea it was to move to California, but I think we both always knew we'd end up there, trying to do something better with our lives. By the time Casey and I made our decision to move, we had just graduated from Anacortes High School. It was the perfect time in our lives to take a chance and see if we could turn our dreams into reality.

For the first trip to San Diego, I had planned to go alone and stay with family friends while Casey stayed behind in Anacortes. I was going to check out the area to see if our dream was even possible while Casey saved up enough money to pay for our move to San Diego a few weeks later. I made the 1,300-mile trip to San Diego and stayed with our family friends, the Malloys, a few days after high school graduation. The Malloy family moved from Anacortes to San Diego a few years earlier so that my friend, Michael Malloy, could play basketball. At my high school, sports were never taken too seriously, so the best athletes often had to move out of the area if they wanted to be competitive.

Before I left for San Diego, I told my family about my decision to become a professional skateboarder. My parents were very supportive, just

*Jake, Donna, and Keith Anderson*

like they always were. My dad, Keith, was highly educated. He was a former Marine and had a doctorate in psychology. He served as a high school counselor and always encouraged me to follow my dreams. I'm sure he was disappointed that I wasn't going to college, but he never tried to change my mind. He knew how much I loved skateboarding and he wanted me to be happy. My mom, Donna, is the most supportive mother you could imagine. She never shied me away from following my heart, so she also encouraged me to go to San Diego. My five older sisters, Megan, Johanna, Wendy, Beth, and Chelsea, also backed my

*Jake Anderson and Casey Rigney*

decision. They knew that if anybody could do something great with skateboarding, it would be Casey and me. They also knew the Malloy family who I would be staying with, which made the trip easier on all of us.

My plan was to stay with the Malloys for about a week. While I was there, I wanted to skate with professionals to see if I was good enough to compete for sponsors. Soon after I arrived, my friend, Cody Malloy, introduced me to local skateboarder, Devin Brankovich. Devin was sponsored by the company *Sixteen Skateboards*, and he knew a lot of professional skateboarders in the area. I skated with them day and night during the week I was there. We'd warm up at Carlsbad Skatepark and then skate at either San Diego City College or Oceanside High School. We'd skate for hours, and the more time I spent with Devin, the more it became apparent that the plan Casey and I had put into motion might actually be possible.

There was one specific time during my trip that I realized I had what it took to be a professional skateboarder. We were at Torrey Pines High School, skating like we always did, and I ollied a set of twenty-one stairs outside the school gym. It was just a little bigger than the shipping containers I used to jump from at the Safeway store in Anacortes, and I didn't think much of it. I had no idea that it was a big deal, and I really didn't care. But Devin's disbelief when I told him that I had ollied the set of twenty-one stairs made me realize, for the first time, that I might actually make it as a professional. No one he knew, professional or otherwise, had ollied those stairs before. He thought I was lying to him. He didn't think what I had done was possible. I remember feeling so full of pride and ego when I left Torrey Pines that day. Looking back now, almost fifteen years later, I see how naïve it was to be so cocky when I had

achieved so little. But I was young and invincible. I thought to myself that turning pro was almost going to be *too easy*. In fact, I thought I'd have to carry Casey on my shoulders for a few years while I became famous.

By the end of my trip, I was anxious to get back to Anacortes to tell Casey what I had experienced. I was going to tell him to quit his job, pack his bags, and head back down to San Diego with me to find sponsors. I felt like a hero because I had traveled to San Diego alone and returned with the news we had dreamed about. The same day I returned to Anacortes—I don't think I had even seen my family yet—Casey and I were already making plans to leave for San Diego the next day. We were on top of the world and nothing could stop us. We went out to skate that night because it had been over a week since we last skated together. We wanted to practice so we'd be ready to impress the sponsors in San Diego. Our normal route was to leave Casey's house, skate down 32nd Street, head toward the Island Hospital, and then circle back around to return home. As we left Casey's house that day, I followed him just like I always did. We bombed the hill on 32nd Street, just like we had done a thousand times before, and we made our way toward the Island Hospital. Between 32nd Street and the hospital, there's a small set of nine stairs that we'd always jump. If you knew me at the time, then you knew that jumping nine stairs was about the equivalent of stepping off a curb. I had jumped those stairs countless times before, so I thought nothing of it. But on that day, for whatever reason, as I started my jump my body turned ninety degrees and my back foot came off the board. This wasn't anything out of the ordinary though, and I still had time to fix my position before I landed. But because my back foot came off the board when I was in mid-air, it meant that when I came back down I wouldn't have control over where I placed it. My foot landed on the very edge of the tail, I slipped off the board, and as I squatted my knees to land, my ankle turned sideways–the way that it shouldn't–and I heard a loud crunch.

It was my left ankle, the one that I used to land. For me, being goofy-footed (my right foot is my lead foot), it was the worst-case scenario. I knew right away it was over. It took only a split second before it sank in that my dreams were finished. As soon as I heard the crunch, I started screaming at Casey. In my mind, on that day, he was the one who convinced *me* to go skateboarding with *him*. It was *me* that was following *him* down 32nd Street and down the set of stairs. I remember screaming, "It's over, it's over, I'm going to fucking kill you! It's over!" I was devastated and in shock. I was in physical pain from landing on my ankle, and I knew that I had just made the worst possible mistake. Casey ran to Island Hospital to get help as I laid on the pavement wondering how I could have let this happen.

Throughout high school, Casey and I always took care of each other. Whether I was sticking up for him at school or he was working to save money so we could move to California together, we always looked out for each other. But from that point forward, starting on the day of my fall, Casey started taking care of me. While Casey was trying to find help at the hospital, the Anacortes police arrived to investigate what happened. For years they had dealt with us causing trouble, but they didn't know the seriousness of my injury or the pain I was in that day. The injury I suffered was a common injury to skateboarders, but it wasn't an injury that was *supposed* to happen to me. When they heard me scream, *"It's over. I'm going to fucking kill you!"* and then looked down from the top of the stairs to see a body lying at the bottom, they assumed I was a murder victim. By the time I explained what happened, Casey had returned from the hospital. I got the help I needed that day, and I can still remember feeling devastated as I realized my skateboarding career was over before it even started. Before that day, I was God in my eyes. There was nothing I couldn't do. Nothing could stop me. But then getting hurt on something like a *nine-stair* quickly brought me back to reality. Soon after, I got a six-inch plate and twelve screws put into my left ankle, and I was officially an ex-skateboarder.

Following my accident, I was a changed person. I was depressed and I didn't snap out of it like others thought I should. If I had just bounced back from my injury I might have saved myself five years of torture. But instead I became withdrawn and hopeless. I had maybe two thousand dollars to my name—money that I had managed to save from salmon fishing each summer—and I had no plan for my future. I felt lost for the first time. I assumed that would be my low point, and I wish that it was, but it only got much worse from there. I never imagined that I was about to spend years of my life battling to get back to where I was the day before my accident.

Not knowing what to do with myself, I did the only thing that made sense—I went to California with Casey like we planned. We didn't have enough money to rent an apartment in San Diego, so we rented a cheap apartment in nearby Escondido, instead. I followed Casey for weeks, watching him skate and talk to sponsors. Part of me was happy for my best friend, but part of me was becoming jealous.

My ankle slowly healed and eventually my cast came off. I got to the point where I should have physically been able to skate again, but it didn't feel the same. When I got on my board, I wasn't seeing what I used to see anymore. To make matters worse, I was getting heavier into drinking and smoking pot, two things that I never used to do before my accident. I'm sure the pot and alcohol had something to do with my weakened skating ability, but it felt like much more than that. I was losing care and slipping deeper into depression every day. It felt like no matter what I did, my life was only getting worse. It didn't help that Casey was skateboarding really well and getting a lot of attention from sponsors. I knew that if I was skating like I did that day at Torrey Pines, just a few months earlier, those same sponsors would be looking at me, too. The more I felt sorry for myself, the more I drank. I got to the point where I was drinking Scotch all day long. I was also smoking more pot, and my twenty dollar a day habit was becoming a forty dollar a day habit.

Meanwhile, Casey was becoming more unlike me every day, in every way. He saw his best friend throwing his life away and it was hard for him to watch. Every morning he would yell at me, "Don't even think about smoking today! We've got shit to do! We gotta skate, we gotta film, we've gotta get sponsors! Get it together." The trouble was, even skateboarding didn't matter to me anymore. I was falling into a hole and giving up on life.

If I knew then what I know now about addiction, I would have clearly seen where I was heading. I would have known that it was going to get a lot worse before it got better. But I assumed that I'd get my life back on track any day. I thought what I was going through was normal, and maybe it was for a time, but then I headed into darker places than I expected. My real downward spiral began when I tried to replace the high I felt from skateboarding with the high from popping Vicodin. I would take a handful of pills and then drink Scotch, and for me it felt like jumping off a huge set of stairs on my skateboard. I would get loaded and see what happened, just like I used to take on a big jump and see if I landed it. I was becoming more self-destructive and making bad decisions every day. I didn't know how to stop and I didn't want to.

The day that changed my life was the day Casey's car was stolen outside our apartment in Escondido. Having your car stolen in Escondido is nothing new, but on that day Casey and I were scheduled to meet with skateboarding sponsors *Arcade Skateboards* and *Autobahn Wheels*. I was going to give skateboarding one last try and it was my chance to redeem myself. When we walked out of our apartment that morning, we saw a long line of cars parked along the side of the street as usual. Every car was in its place except for Casey's Honda Accord. His car was nowhere to be found; it had apparently been stolen the night before. That meant we didn't have a ride to meet the sponsors, and I saw it as the perfect excuse to go back inside and smoke pot. So I gave up and returned to the apartment while Casey found a ride to meet the sponsors. It was on that day that Casey signed his first professional skateboarding contract with *Arcade Skateboards*. He finally achieved his high school dream and became a professional skateboarder. Casey deserved a lot of credit. He was a disciplined athlete who worked hard every day to achieve his dreams. That was the difference between us back then. He would fight and keep moving forward, no matter what, while I looked for any excuse to take the easy way out.

I couldn't hide the fact that I was jealous of Casey's success. He was having a lot of fun and meeting new people, and I started to think that I was weighing him down. I was falling into the role of the weed-smoking-drunk-buddy who could kind of

*Casey Rigney*

skate, but wasn't really serious about it. That's what I started putting into my own head more and more. I didn't know how self-destructive those thoughts could be. During this time, I was slowly finding out that I was human. A lot of the skateboarding tricks I was known for required me to believe that I was superhuman. To jump off fourteen foot platforms and to do flips off stairs, I had to believe that I was the best. But once I found out that I was just as breakable as everybody else, all the magic went away from skateboarding. I was just another guy trying to do the job. And if I didn't have skateboarding, I didn't have anything.

By the time I was twenty-two, I was totally withdrawn from skateboarding. I didn't have dreams of making it as a pro anymore, and I felt like a different person. I was still in San Diego, now living off Casey, and I was getting heavy into cocaine. One night, while I was at a party, someone convinced me that if I tried methamphetamine, it would make me want to skate again. And I wanted to *want* to skate again. It made sense to me at the time. So I tried meth, and it's a decision that I wish I could take back. Once I tried the drug, my life was never the same. I hated the drug, but I loved how it made me feel. I ended up doing meth for a few days straight and within a week it completely overpowered me.

Even though my life was unravelling, Casey never stopped taking care of me. He was the only positive influence I had in California, and he tried to convince me to stop using meth by reminding me how much I loved skateboarding. But nothing but the drug mattered to me anymore. I couldn't be helped and I didn't want to change. I only wanted the drug. Eventually, I ended up moving back to Anacortes because I ran out of money and I was becoming destructive to Casey's career. He cared so much about me that he was willing to risk everything to take care of me, but I cared so little for him that I wasn't willing to give up drugs to save our friendship.

Soon after I returned to Anacortes, while I was still twenty-two, I was arrested for negligent driving and lost my driver's license for two years. Looking back, I can say with confidence that being arrested saved my life. It was the best thing that ever happened to me. The judge sentenced me to thirty days of substance abuse treatment at the Lakeside-Milam Recovery Center in Seattle. I'll never forget my time at Lakeside-Milam because it's when I found out that I was a drug addict. It was clear to everyone around me that I was an addict, but I wasn't willing to accept it. I was only willing to accept that I was an alcoholic. In fact, I was proud to be an alcoholic, but I refused to be a drug addict. From the moment I walked into the facility, though, I was told, "You Are A Drug Addict." After a few days at Lakeside-Milam, I was beginning to withdraw from drugs. I was desperate to go home, so I said to my doctors, *"I'm thinking about killing myself."* I knew that by threatening suicide, they would be forced to transfer me to the alternative treatment program, known as the "dual diagnosis program." The dual diagnosis program lasts for only eight days, while my current treatment program was scheduled to last for thirty days. Unlike the Lakeside-Milam program, the dual diagnosis program focused half its treatment on mental problems (treated at Fairfax Hospital) and half on substance abuse problems (treated at Lakeside-Milam). By manipulating my way into the dual diagnosis program, I knew that I'd be released sooner so I could return to my addiction. Today, I know that I should have stayed at Lakeside-Milam to get fully treated. Part of me believes that if I had stayed all thirty days, I might have broken my addiction years sooner than I did. But at the time, I was very selfish and I decided to manipulate my way into the alternative treatment program so I could end my sentence sooner.

Even though I left early, I managed to learn a few things during my eight days in treatment. Mainly I learned about withdrawal. I found out why I was so sick all the time and couldn't get out of bed. I also learned that my feelings of withdrawal were only temporary. I started to understand what being an alcoholic really meant by finding out that I was a drug addict. Before my stay at Lakeside-Milam, I thought being an alcoholic was like wearing a badge of honor. All the best skateboarders and fishermen were alcoholics, and I wanted to be just like them. I thought drug addicts were the scum of the earth. When I learned that I was a drug addict, I found out how dire my situation really was. I saw that my chances of survival were slim. So when I got out of treatment, I decided to make a fresh start and get clean, but I didn't even last a day before I relapsed. In fact, following my stay at Lakeside-Milam, I stole from my parents for the first time. I took twenty dollars from my dad's wallet and bought drugs.

*Even when my addiction was at its worst, I managed to stay sober while I salmon fished each summer. I went to Bristol Bay, Alaska, every summer since I was seventeen, and no matter what was happening in my life, I fished for salmon. I would experience terrible withdrawal, but I would get a temporary break from my problems. I would become sick, shit my pants, and barely be able to get out of bed, but I would manage to do my job and stay clean for those few weeks. Fishing was my only safe haven for many years.*

Lakeside-Milam also taught me a valuable lesson about how my addiction impacted my family. I became ashamed and guilt stricken of who I had become and what I had done to the people I loved. I felt like a victim and I knew I was toxic. I was so scared that I would cause more trouble for my family that I started living on the streets. I didn't want to hurt anybody anymore. I thought the only safe place I had *was* the street. I knew that my chances of leading a normal life were zero because I was so heavy into meth and I didn't know how to stop. In fact, I never thought I'd survive past the age of twenty-five. In my mind, I was doomed to death and I didn't want my family to watch me slowly kill myself.

I stayed on the streets for most of the day and night for nearly two years. It was the longest two years of my life. I was always on the move and I never slept. I would skateboard all day and all night, or I would just walk around the city. I was forced by the drug to keep moving. Sometimes I would sneak into my parents' house early in the morning to recover, but I refused to see them. I was too ashamed of myself and I hated what I had become.

Throughout my addiction, my parents never stopped loving me. They pleaded with me to come home during the two years I lived on the streets. Everybody outside my family would tell them to kick me out and to not have anything to do with me, but my mom and dad were always willing to take me back in. The reason I lived on the streets was because I couldn't put myself around people I loved. My biggest regret is what I put my dad through. He had a doctorate degree in psychology and was formally trained to help others overcome addiction. He understood my disease, and he knew that as a parent he couldn't control whether I'd use drugs. He knew that he could yell at me, punish me, and banish me, but I'd stop using only when I made the decision for myself.

My battle against meth addiction continued until 2004, when I was twenty-four years old. At that time, I was out of money and I realized that if I didn't straighten up my life, I would end up either dead or in jail. That was the turning point for me. It was the first time in my adult life that I *wanted* to change. I still had no idea *how* to change, but I knew that I had to try something different. So I did the only thing that made sense to me at the time; I moved. I decided to go find Casey and reconnect with the one person who I could always depend on. I knew that he wouldn't turn me away, despite all that I had put him through. But Casey was no longer living in San Diego. He had moved out east to Washington, D.C., because that was the new popular skating spot. When I arrived in D.C., Casey took me in and let me live in his townhouse while I tried to get clean. He knew that I was serious about quitting drugs because he could see that I was scared.

What I remember most about my three months in D.C. is always feeling sick. I was withdrawing from meth and I didn't understand what my body was going through. I had learned a lot about withdrawal while I was at Lakeside-Milam, but I wasn't prepared to feel sick all day, every day. When Casey saw how sick I was, he refused to leave me alone. He started bringing me with him everywhere he skated. One time, he and the other professional skateboarders from the east coast were filming a skate video that was being shot by digital media producer, Chris Hall. They drove around D.C. in a white conversion van, going from one skate spot to the next. I tagged along, and when we'd arrive at each location, Chris would film the skaters and I would find a park bench to sleep on. In one of the videos, you could see a homeless person sleeping on a bench in the background, and I was sleeping right next to him. His feet were right beside my face but I was too sick to care. On the video, you can hear Chris say, *"portable bum..."* under his breath as the camera zoomed in on me. From that day on, I was known as the "portable bum" in D.C.

The time I spent in D.C. let me reconnect with Casey and break my addiction to meth. The last time I used the substance was 2004. I couldn't have given up the drug without Casey's help. From the day I broke my ankle to the day I broke my addiction, Casey was always there for me. As I started to get my strength back, I began to miss my family. It was only after I got clean that I started to understand the consequences of my addiction. I knew that I had put my family through hell, and I wanted to start rebuilding our relationship.

When I returned to Anacortes, I started believing in myself again. I was finally making smart decisions and I wanted to support myself. I was only fishing for a few weeks out of the year, so I needed to find a steady job. I turned to my friend's dad, Rick Durphee, who took a chance on me and

*Keith and Jake Anderson*

gave me a job painting houses. Rick and I would drive around from 7 a.m. to 6 p.m. painting houses and adding spray texture to walls. He changed my life by encouraging me to join an addiction support program. I had been told time and again that I should join a program, but Rick made me see that if I got help, I could live a better life. He may not have understood my drug addiction, but Rick made me see that I had a way out.

As I continued my recovery, I started to realize how much I admired my dad. He was an educated and respected member of the community, and I wanted to be more like him. He had watched me relapse countless times, but he was always patient. He always trusted that I'd find my own path to sobriety. I wanted to repay my dad for the support he had given me, so with him in mind I went to my first support group meeting. From the very beginning, I believed in the program and followed it without question. I said to my counselors, "Fine, if you want me to go to ninety meetings in ninety days, I will." I was working the program, and with the help of my family I had finally overcome my five-year addiction to drugs and alcohol.

# 2

# Greenhorn

Fishing saved my life. No matter what drug I was addicted to, or what problem I was facing, the time I spent fishing always brought me peace. It let me escape from my addiction. I had to be sober to fish, it was too dangerous not to be. Fishing made me focus on what I was doing at that moment and nothing more. I couldn't bring any other thoughts into it. I had to focus on holding onto the pot, opening the door of the pot, sorting the crab, stacking the pot, and then doing it all over again. If I didn't concentrate on the task at hand, I would get hurt or die. Fishing kept my mind focused on one thing at a time, and it let me forget my addiction. Without fishing, I could not have survived.

Growing up, I loved skateboarding but I admired fishermen. When I was eight years old, my best friend was Kyle Crews, and his dad, Ken, was a king crabber. I remember seeing Ken return from crab fishing in Alaska and he always seemed scary to me. He had a giant sense of humor and he looked real tough. To me, Ken personified everything that a king crabber was. I wanted to be just like him. I wanted to be tough, and tough looking. I grew up with that image of Kyle's dad in my mind, and he inspired me to become a crab fisherman.

Fishing has always been in my blood. My dad fished every summer, and so did my uncle Brian Mavar, his brother Nick, and their father, Nick Mavar, Sr. We called Nick Mavar, Sr., "Dida," which is Croatian for grandpa. He wasn't my blood grandpa, but I always considered him to be. Brian, Nick, and Dida fished together for over thirty years in the Bering Sea. As a young boy, I would beg them to take me fishing in Alaska, but they'd never allow it. I was too small and they told me I'd have to wait for my chance.

*(Back row, from left) Alec Mavar, Brian Mavar, Nick Mavar, Sr., Nick Mavar, Jr. (Front row, from left) Tyson Mavar, Jake Anderson, John Mavar*

Finally, when I was seventeen years old I got my first chance to fish in Alaska. My brother-in-law, Jessie Brown, who normally fished salmon every summer in Bristol Bay, decided to leave his job on the fishing vessel (F/V) *Sunny C*, and he gave me his open spot. I survived my first season and I've never looked back. I didn't think fishing would turn into my career, but I liked how I could earn enough money fishing in the summer to support my skateboarding in the winter.

*(From left) Jake Anderson, Alec Mavar, Tyson Mavar*

*Jake Anderson and Tyson Mavar*

I continued to fish salmon every summer until I was twenty years old, at which time I got a job as a processor on a factory trawler. It was the F/V *Alaska Ocean*, and we fished pollock under captain Scott Symonds. I started at the very bottom, literally, working in the boat's factory. I was a driver, which meant that I shoved fish into a filet machine for twelve hours a day. I wanted to work my way upstairs onto the deck, but it was important that I did it without my family's influence. So I busted my ass, working long shifts in the factory and then volunteering to work on deck after my shift was over. I would help the deckhands any way that I could. All that mattered to me was being a part of their group. By my second season on the *Alaska Ocean*, I had worked my way up from the factory into the galley. I was a dishwasher, and after I'd work my twelve hour shift in the galley, I'd once again go upstairs to help the crew on deck. Sometimes I'd work for thirty-six hours straight and then sleep for a few hours. That continued for a few seasons, but I never did get a job on the deck of the *Alaska Ocean*. The owner hired a relative to fill the position and it was a very humbling experience.

I don't regret my time on the *Alaska Ocean* because it helped me develop a good reputation and strong work ethic. Just after I left the *Alaska Ocean*, in 2005, my uncle Brian got me a job fishing cod aboard the F/V *Nuka Island* out of Kodiak, Alaska. It was my first time cod fishing, and it was an experience I'll never forget. I had never worked on a pot fishing boat before, and weighing only 135 pounds made the job nearly impossible. Every day aboard the *Nuka Island* was a learning experience. My hands hurt, my knees hurt, and my back hurt throughout the entire season. The job almost killed me and I told myself I'd never pot fish again.

Following my first cod season on the *Nuka Island*, I was invited back to do a tender season for herring. It turned out to be the worst season of my life. I contracted a dangerous staph infection in my throat, leg, and stomach. I also damaged my rotator cuff and had to be hospitalized. Not only did I get injured, but I didn't make any money. I always took advice from my uncle Brian, so I called him from my hospital bed and asked, "So how does this work? We don't make money the first year we're pot fishermen, and then we make

a ton of money the second year?" He replied, "What? You didn't make any money? Get on a plane right now. Don't call anybody. Just get on a plane and come home." As soon as I was released from the hospital, I followed my uncle's instructions and flew home to recover.

While I was at home, I fell back into my old ways again. I relapsed. To deal with the pain from my rotator cuff injury, I was prescribed Vicodin. I used the medication responsibly at first, but before long I was eating pain pills just like I did two years earlier. In my mind, I was *not* an addict again. I was just taking my medication. But when I ran out of Vicodin and started buying it on the street, I knew I had lost my way again. I kept my relapse silent because I didn't want to disappoint my family. I also didn't want my addiction to affect my fishing career. I knew that no matter how bad my drug dependency was, if I could just make it to the next fishing season I'd be able to get clean and turn the corner.

My next opportunity to fish came a few months later, in 2006, when my uncle Brian got me a job fishing king crab with him, Rick McLeod, and Brad Parker on the F/V *Mark I*. If I had never endured that terrible herring season on the *Nuka*

*Brian Mavar*

*Island,* I wouldn't have earned the reputation and respect that allowed me to fish with my uncle Brian on the *Mark I.* My uncle was notorious for *not* giving recommendations to other fishermen. He didn't go out of his way to vouch for others because it risked tarnishing his own reputation. So it meant a lot that my uncle Brian not only recommended me to the company that he worked for, but he recommended me for the specific boat that he worked on. We caught one hundred thousand pounds of king crab that season and it was back-breaking work. The *Mark I* wasn't set up for crabbing. It was a trawler converted to a crabber for a season, so there wasn't high tech equipment on board for crabbing. What made that season so memorable was that I got to work alongside Rick McLeod and Brad Parker, who were both former engineers on the F/V *Northwestern*. Rick and Brad would tell me stories about the *Northwestern* and what it was like to work on the best boat in the fleet. They would tell me how the crew never slept, hardly ate, and worked around the clock. They made me afraid of that boat because they talked about it with such pride and admiration.

At the end of the crab season, when the *Mark I* was sitting at Trident Dock in Dutch Harbor, Alaska, I saw the *Northwestern* for the first time. The two boats were docked next to each other and they were sitting stern to stern. Since they're both house forward boats, I had a clear view inside the *Northwestern*. I remember taking pictures and calling my friends to brag about how I was next to the legendary boat. Although my uncle Nick Mavar worked on the *Northwestern*, I was still star struck by it. The boat was not yet well known countrywide or worldwide, but it was respected by crab fishermen. It was the best boat you could possibly work on. The same day we docked, the *Mark I* needed fresh water so I was sent to the *Northwestern* to borrow a garden hose. I remem-

ber calling my friends afterwards and telling them how I had *actually* borrowed a garden hose from the *Northwestern*. It was a privilege to even step foot on that boat.

At that same time, in late 2006, there started to be talk in the fleet that Sig Hansen, captain of the *Northwestern*, was looking to hire a greenhorn for the upcoming 2007 opilio crab season. Between my uncle Nick working on the *Northwestern*, and having just finished a season with Rick McLeod and Brad Parker, there was word that I might be offered the job. But after completing the cod season on the *Nuka Island* and the king crab season on the *Mark I*, I had no will to pot fish ever again. I was absolutely horrible at it. I could barely make it through the day, and by the end of the season I didn't have enough energy to prepare bait on time, let alone sort crab.

If I was offered the greenhorn position on the *Northwestern*, though, my uncle Brian and my uncle Nick were going to make sure that I took the job. At that point in my life, they were in charge of my fishing career. I didn't know what the best decisions were for my future, so they took it upon themselves to decide for me. They came to the conclusion that I should fish on the *Northwestern* if given the chance. But I was reluctant to leave the *Mark I* because, honestly, I was afraid of the *Northwestern*. The opportunity seemed overwhelming. I didn't think that I could fish a million pounds of opies or 460,000 pounds of king crab, which was their normal quota at the time. But I always did what my uncles said, especially my uncle Brian. He was a few years older than Nick, so even Nick took his advice. The common joke between Nick and I was, "I'm going to tell uncle Brian on you!" Whatever Brian said, I did. I didn't argue, that's just how it went.

Sig offered me the opilio job in early 2007, and I was scared to death before the season began. I knew that TV cameras would be filming the crew all season long, but that didn't bother me because I was used to being filmed when I skateboarded. Instead, I was scared of the expectations that came with fishing on the most respected boat in the fleet. But I had already pot fished for king crab and cod, so in my eyes I was by no means a greenhorn. Instead, I considered myself to be a fisherman in a new fishery. I definitely *was not* a greenhorn though. But as soon as I threw my bags on board the *Northwestern* to begin the season, I found out that I was going to be treated *exactly* like a greenhorn.

The first words spoken to me by deck boss Edgar Hansen were, "Welcome to Hell." After my greeting, nobody on the crew would shake my hand. That was a greenhorn tradition that I didn't like. Not getting a handshake was hard for me to accept, and it really pissed me off. But I tried my best to stay focused on the big picture. To me, the season was about proving myself as a deckhand and making my uncle Nick and my uncle Brian proud. While I didn't manage to get a handshake from the crew, I *did* manage to get the brunt of

*Edgar Hansen*

everything bad that happened on the boat. If we weren't on the crab, it was *Jake's bad luck.* If I opened a bag of potato chips upside down—something you're never supposed to do on the *Northwestern*—nobody would talk to me for the rest of the day. If I was slow baiting a pot, I was castrated.

It took nearly the entire season to learn the superstitions of the boat, and some of them were hard to get used to. For example, if a crew member opened a bag of chips upside down, he had to immediately dump the chips into a Ziploc bag or throw them into a bowl. If Sig came down from the wheelhouse and found chips in a Ziploc bag, then he knew that somebody had opened the chips upside down. He would literally come unglued. Or, if Sig saw a can of beans or a can of soup upside down, he would lose his mind. There were other rules, too, like no cowboy boots, no pictures of horses, and no bananas on the boat. These superstitions became ingrained in me and I didn't mind them once I knew what they were. In fact, I like the traditions. They have been around long before Sig, and I think it's important to honor them.

During my first opie season on the *Northwestern*, my goal wasn't to earn full share, operate the crane, or run the hydraulics. It was a lot more basic than that. I wanted to throw the hook, tie the stack down, and prepare bait. In fact, the most important job on deck is reserved for the greenhorn, and it's preparing bait. Chopping bait, filling bait bags, counting bait bags, and making sure there is always enough bait–those are the responsibilities that ultimately determine if a boat will catch crab or not. For the entire season, I tried to never get too excited when the crab pots came up

*(From left) Norman Hansen, Nick Mavar, Jake Anderson*

full, and I tried to never get too depressed when they came up empty. I tried to enjoy whatever task I was doing and I did my best to stay in the moment. I figured we'll fill the tanks when we fill the tanks, we'll get home when we get home, and so on.

Toward the end of my first opie season, I had no idea what Sig was planning to do with me. I didn't know if he was going to invite me back for another season, or if the crew would even want to work with me again. I wouldn't know if I was accepted by Sig and his crew until it came time for me to get—or not get—my boat jacket. I begged and pleaded for a *Northwestern* jacket every day I was on the boat. I knew that if I received a jacket, then my job was secure and I had found my new home. It would mean that I could do pretty much whatever I wanted on the boat, and I would always have a job the following season. But it was a double-edged sword. The jacket meant that I couldn't be fired, but it also meant that I could never leave. When Sig finally gave me the jacket off his back on the last day of opie season, it made every cold, hungry, tired, lonely, and scared day all worth it. Tears actually poured down my face when Sig handed me his jacket because it meant that I was *somebody*. It didn't mean that I had a fishing job, it meant that I had a fishing *career*.

For weeks following the first opie season, I ran all over Seattle doing chores for Sig. It was part of an old Norwegian tradition that was started by Sig's father, Sverre. I would hear stories of the entire crew doing chores for the "old man," as they called him. The crew would stain the overhang on his house, mow his lawn, and do whatever he wanted. Back then, you didn't ask questions, you just did what the old man said. So when Sig took

*Sig Hansen*

on that tradition with me, I wasn't going to say no. Whether he wanted me to prune his trees, take down Christmas lights, or run errands to the accounting office, I did it. I think that's why Matt Bradley, Edgar, and some of the other veterans from the *Northwestern* accused me of kissing Sig's ass. But I didn't care. I understood that you always take care of your captain, you always take care of your boat owner, and you always take care of your senior fishermen. Besides, when somebody does for you what Sig has done for me, you don't say "no" when he asks you to take out his garbage.

During my second year on the *Northwestern*, Edgar trimmed the fat on all the mistakes I had made during my first year. He also worked with me on tying knots and doing gear work. He made me earn the right to move up, and he still didn't let me stack pots, run hydraulics, or operate the crane. It was clear to me by my second year that I was on *Edgar's deck*. Edgar was in charge of all engineering and deck operations, and Sig was in charge of overseeing the entire boat operation. There was a clear division of labor. Sig ran everything upstairs, and Edgar ran everything downstairs. So, if I wanted to advance on deck, it was only going to be if Edgar allowed it. I begged him to let me do anything more than what I was already doing on deck, but Edgar kept me in check. I always wanted to do my job plus *one more thing* like run hydraulics or operate the crane, but Edgar said that teaching me would have slowed the entire operation to a halt, so he made me wait.

It wasn't until my third year on the *Northwestern*, in 2009, that I started learning how to stack pots and run hydraulics. Within a few weeks I had built my confidence to a level where I could easily

*(From left) Nick Mavar, Matt Bradley, Jake Anderson*

stack a full load of pots in any kind of weather. I finally reached the point where I was able to do every job on deck. My fishing career had never looked brighter. But then, on February 13th, 2009, halfway through opie season, I received a call from home that forever changed my life. It was something that I wasn't prepared for. The news was devastating. My older sister, Chelsea, had unexpectedly passed away.

# My Sister, Chelsea

My sister, Chelsea, was a rocker. She was a child of the '80s, and she loved hair bands like *Bon Jovi*, *Poison*, and *Warrant*. She wore a black leather jacket and had big poofy hair with a wave in the front. She was eight years older than me and I admired her. When I was young, Chelsea would let me watch scary movies with her like *Friday the 13th* and *A Nightmare on Elm Street*. As I grew older, she became someone I could always trust and we became inseparable. By the time I was in high school, Chelsea and I were spending hours together after school going for long drives in her old Ford Trio. She was so much fun to hang

*Chelsea Anderson*

out with because there were never any expectations with her. When I was with my other friends,
we were either skateboarding or going to parties,
and there was always an expectation that we had
to be *doing* something. But with Chelsea, it didn't
matter what we were doing, it was always fun.
We'd start driving in her car, and we'd just keep
going. We'd never ask each other, "Should we turn
around now?" or "Where should we go next?" Instead, we'd just keep driving and it didn't matter

where we were going. When you were with Chelsea, it was always all right, whatever you were doing. That's what I loved most about my sister.

Chelsea grew up differently than everybody else. When she was two years old, she developed rheumatoid arthritis. She would hurt so bad that she would cry, and some days she could barely move. She was in and out of Seattle Children's Hospital her entire childhood. My parents were heartbroken because their daughter was in constant pain and there was nothing they could do to stop it. Her arthritis was so severe that she wasn't expected to live past the age of twelve. But Chelsea defied the doctors. The most remarkable thing

*Chelsea and Keith Anderson*

about my sister was that even though she was constantly hurting, she never complained. When her arthritis left her confined to her bed and in so much pain that she couldn't walk, she never complained. When her arthritis progressed, she never complained about getting the shit beat out of her every day by her awful disease. That was the life my sister endured. She was in endless pain, but she never let it hold her back. She always pushed through.

As Chelsea grew older, her physical and mental condition continued to decline. She wasn't the same person she used to be. By the time she reached her mid-thirties, she had developed abscesses all over her body and she began to suffer from recurring bouts of pneumonia. My family would pray and plead all the time to keep Chelsea alive. She was only expected to live to age twelve, and I feel like we held her hostage for the last ten years of her life because we wanted so badly to keep her with us.

The day Chelsea passed was a day I'll never forget. It was Friday, February 13th, 2009, and I was fishing opies on the *Northwestern*. We were just a few weeks into the season when a phone call came into the wheelhouse. I was standing on deck with my uncle Nick, when Norman Hansen approached us and said, "Nick, you have a phone call. It's kind of an emergency..." I thought it was strange that Norman used the word "emergency" to describe Nick's phone call. On a boat, especially in the Bering Sea, you never want to arouse suspicion to the crew that something's wrong. Words like "emergency" are not used lightly. As Nick went to the wheelhouse to take the call, the boat began a ten mile run to the crab pots. The crew used the hour long break as a chance to sleep, but I was wide awake wondering about the purpose of Nick's call. When the hour was up, the crew awoke, we put on our gear and returned to the deck. The wind was blowing about forty knots that day and it was just nasty. It's easily fished in, but it's not very fun to be on deck. So we were outside, waiting for Sig to tell us that we were approaching the first buoy bag. And we waited...and we waited... We could tell that Sig was just jogging. We weren't making way through the water and we weren't hitting the buoy bags. Slowly, half an hour went by and we were still waiting. Nick hadn't returned from the wheelhouse yet, and I started to worry that Nick's dad, Dida, may have passed away. The more I thought about the possibilities, the more I started to panic. I realized that the emergency phone call could have been for either Nick *or me*. I knew that if my family had bad news to tell me, they would filter it through Nick first. My mom was always very protective of what information I received and when I received it. She knew my history with addiction and she always feared that I might lose control again. So if there was important news to tell me she would run it by Nick first, and then allow him to break it to me when the time was right. Finally, after another thirty minutes of waiting, Nick came down from the wheelhouse and confirmed my worst fears. The bad news was for me. My sister, Chelsea, had unexpectedly passed away. It was Friday the 13th, and it was the worst day of my life.

When Nick broke the news to me, I lost control. I broke down, and I was pretty loud about it. I was twenty-eight years old and becoming more conscious of life. The news of my sister's passing crushed me because I knew what it would do to my family. I went to the wheelhouse and made the difficult call home. When my mom told me that Chelsea died from pneumonia, my first thoughts were that she's no longer in pain and she's now in a better place. My next thought was that I have to

*Chelsea with her nephew, Thomas Lawrence*

be strong for my family because they're depending
on me.

Deciding to let TV cameras film my phone call
home was an easy choice for me. I could have said
to the producers, *No, I'm not letting you film this.
I'm not going to talk about it. It's too personal.* But
then I thought about Chelsea. She was such an
amazing friend and sister, and I was going to be
damned if I was going to rob the world of getting
to know her like I did. Everybody in Chelsea's life
was better for knowing her, and the audience de-

served to see what a selfless, courageous person she was. I also thought about what Chelsea always told me she wanted, which was to be remembered. It felt only natural to do what I could to honor my sister.

After I talked to my family, I sat down with Sig to discuss the rest of the season. I said to him, "I can finish this trip. I'll be fine. I'll make it through, and when we're done I'll go to town and take the first plane home." There was still a month or two left in the opie season and I didn't want the crew to work shorthanded. But Sig was concerned about my safety, so he turned the boat around and headed for Saint Paul Island. Even though I resisted, there was no way he was going to let me fish another minute with my sister having just passed away. Sig's decision showed how he always took care of his crew. The most amazing thing you'll see as a sailor is how willing everybody is to come together for one person, no matter who that person is. It's inspiring to see what all mariners will do to help a person in need.

When we arrived at Saint Paul, the first person I saw was my friend, Phil Harris. He gave me a huge hug, told me everything would be ok, and encouraged me to stay strong for my family. Jake

*Phil Harris and Jake Anderson, February 14th, 2009*

*Jake Anderson and Jake Harris, February 14th, 2009*

and Josh Harris were there too, and they gave me their support and told me how sorry they were for my loss. It's amazing how things managed to line up after my sister's passing to keep me safe and out of harm's way. My uncle Nick was on board to break the news to me. Sig and the crew of the *Northwestern* were there to safely get me to Saint Paul Island. Then, meeting Phil, Jake, and Josh Harris when I arrived at Saint Paul made it a lot easier to deal with the pain I was feeling. I wasn't in a sound state of mind, but I knew I'd be okay as I left my Bering Sea family and returned to my real family.

When I arrived home I saw the catastrophic effect that Chelsea's death had on my family, and especially my dad. For her entire life, my dad worried about Chelsea. He cared for her, supported her, and possibly even loved her more. Because she had gone through so much, he always felt like he owed her more than he could give her. I remember seeing my dad cry for the first time during the drive home from her funeral. He never showed weakness before, but he cried uncontrollably that day. He thought it was his fault that Chelsea had rheumatoid arthritis, and he blamed himself for not taking away her pain. There was nothing he could do to give back to Chelsea what the disease had stolen from her. When I saw my dad cry that day, I could see that he was consumed by his grief. He was a changed man. I didn't know it at the time, but I only had a few short months left on earth with my dad. In less than a year, I'd be reliving my worst fears as I mourned his death, too.

# 21-Gun Salute

My dad, Keith Anderson, was a Marine, a psychologist, an author, a cancer survivor, and a fisherman. He was born in the summer of 1947, in Anacortes, Washington. When he was nineteen years old, he met my mom, Donna, on a beach in Anacortes. Growing up, they'd tell me the story of how my mom didn't like my dad at first, but he kept pestering her until she finally gave in and agreed to go on a date with him. They married soon after in July of 1966. Just about the same time my parents married, my dad joined the Marines. He joined right after high school because he had a passion for the Corps and he wanted to serve his country. His brother, Chris Anderson, who served in the Coast Guard at the time, later joined the Marines and flew F-4 Phantoms in the Vietnam War. Together, they selflessly defended our country and showed me the importance of true character and honor.

When my dad was in his mid-twenties, he was honorably discharged from the Marines and then attended college to study psychology. He attended school for twelve years, up until the time I was six years old. He attended the University of Washington, Seattle University, and Western Washington University, where he earned his doctorate degree in psychology. During that time, he and my mom raised me and my five sisters.

*(Back row, from left) Beth, Keith, Donna, Wendy Anderson*
*(Front row, from left) Chelsea, Bilbo, Johanna Anderson*

*Keith and Donna Anderson*

Following college, my dad became a high school counselor. He wanted to provide the community of Anacortes with an inexpensive, professional service that helped people. That's why he chose to become a school counselor and not the owner of his own private practice. I was always proud of my dad for the decision he made to help his community. His gift was counseling, and I experienced it firsthand. When I started to slip into addiction, he would punish me, but at the same time he would also counsel me and help me figure out what was wrong within myself. He would pick me apart, but not like the average parent. He wouldn't talk that much. Instead, he would listen to my complaints and then help me find the answer to my problem without directly telling me what it was. As I continued to struggle with drugs and alcohol, I know that it broke my dad's heart. He was a counselor, but he found himself unable to prevent his own son from abusing drugs. It wasn't his fault though, and one of my biggest regrets is what I put him through when I was at the height of my addiction. Through his education and training, my dad had a genuine understanding of the disease of addiction. He knew that the parent or care provider could not control the addict. He knew that yelling at me, telling me I had to change, and pushing me away wouldn't make me stop using drugs. Instead, it would only push me further into substance abuse. So instead of kicking me out of his house and forcing me to steal, cheat, or do other damaging things, he decided to keep his son around and just *be my dad.* In my support group, they might consider him to be an enabler, but it's not true. If my dad hadn't done exactly what he did, the way that he did it, I would have never managed to break my addiction. My dad's style of parenting was perfect for what I went through. It made me the person that I am today.

The best summer of my life was the summer I spent fishing with my dad in Bristol Bay, Alaska. It was June 2004, and my dad and I fished salmon aboard the F/V *Miss Colleen* for five weeks along with Nick Mavar, Sr. We caught nearly one hundred thousand pounds of product that summer, but it was a tough season. Both my dad and Nick, Sr. were getting older, and line fishing was becoming too physically demanding for them. As fun as it was to fish alongside my dad, it was difficult, too, because it was during that summer that I saw the physical toll that years of fishing had taken on him. He was fifty-seven years old and developing severe pains in his hands and knees. He was also suffering from debilitating migraines that had to be treated with Demerol shots. Demerol is a narcotic pain reliever similar to morphine that he had to inject daily. I watched as my dad battled through constant pain, but just like Chelsea he never complained. He simply fished, did his job, and when he was done fishing for the day he would lay down and take his Demerol. As hard as it was to watch, it was also inspiring. Here was my dad, in so much physical pain, but fighting through it each day with a smile.

*(From left) Nick Mavar, Sr., Keith Anderson, and Jake Anderson aboard the F/V Miss Colleen*

*Keith Anderson*

*Jake Anderson*

*Keith and Jake Anderson*

*Keith Anderson*

My dad's body was breaking down because I don't think he ever fully recovered from his colon cancer diagnosis a few years earlier. At the time of his diagnosis, in 2001, I was fishing pollock on the *Alaska Ocean*. My family didn't tell me about my dad's cancer until I returned home. I was struggling with drugs and alcohol at the time, and I was also young and very selfish. My mom knew that I was dealing with my own issues so she tried to spare me bad news while I was fishing. By the time I returned home and found out about my dad's illness, he had already beaten the cancer and was on his road to recovery. But he wasn't the same person after his year long bout with colon cancer.

By 2008, my dad's migraines became so severe that he had to retire from his counseling job at Anacortes High School. He also suffered a torn rotator cuff that summer, so he had to give up salmon fishing, too. It was at that time that I could see my dad slowly starting to lose his way, just like I did years before when I injured myself skateboarding. All the purpose in his life was changing, and everything he had ever known was now different. I could relate to what my dad was experiencing. When I broke my ankle and couldn't skateboard anymore, I spiraled into drugs and depression. My dad was experiencing the same feelings of loss, but at age sixty-one instead of nineteen. I watched as his mental state deteriorated to the point that he was no longer the same dad that I grew up with. He started to develop sleeping problems and anxiety, for which he was prescribed medication, and then to cope with the pain from his torn rotator cuff, he was prescribed Vicodin. When my dad started combining pharmaceuticals, in addition to the Demerol that he was already taking, things started to turn truly bad for him.

Eventually my dad's prescription to Vicodin ran out, but he still needed the medication to deal with his chronic pain. So my dad started going out on the street to buy pain pills. That was the turning point for my dad and I blame myself for not stopping him. I was addicted to Vicodin at the same time, so I was in no position to offer advice. From the time I injured myself fishing on the *Nuka Island* in 2005 until the time I gained my sobriety in July of 2009, I abused painkillers. I regret my addiction and wish that I could erase my mistakes, but instead all I can do is live each day to distance myself from the last time I used.

My relationship with my dad devolved to the point that he depended on me to supply him with Vicodin. I agreed to help my dad because I could see that he was in severe physical pain. One night, I couldn't find Vicodin but I was offered Oxycontin instead. Oxycontin is a lot stronger than Vicodin and even more addictive. Without giving it any thought, I gave the Oxycontin to my dad and he took the drug for the first time. I crossed a moral boundary within myself that day, and I wish I could take it back. Not too long after my dad tried Oxycontin, his life completely changed. His whole existence started to revolve around the drug. Every time we would have a conversation it always ended up being about Oxycontin. I was addicted to painkillers too, but I *did not* want to talk about drugs. Throughout my whole experience with drugs, I didn't want to hear about them, I didn't want to see them, and I didn't want to be around them. I was disgusted and repulsed by drugs. So when my dad would try to talk to me about Oxycontin, I'd say, *"Dad, what the fuck? Do we really have to talk about Oxycontin again? I really don't want to talk about it."* But no matter what, our conversations always ended up going back to the cotton.

This was a surreal time in my life. Here was the one person that I could always talk to–the one person that when I talked to him, I knew everything would be all right–and he had become an addict. I had faith in my dad like I had faith in God. He always had the answers to all my problems, and now he was ill. It was painful to watch my dad in the state he was in because he was an educated man whose expertise was counseling others to overcome addiction, but he was unable to help himself. I saw that my dad was human and he wasn't Superman anymore.

As my dad's addiction grew stronger, our relationship continued to change. I started to become the father and he became the son. Our role reversal was complete in July of 2009 when I finally broke my addiction to painkillers and started attending addiction support group meetings once again. I went from taking ten Oxycontins per day at my worst to putting no drugs or alcohol into my system of any kind. I was putting my life back together and I began to counsel my dad just like he used to counsel me.

Once I became sober I started to understand that Oxycontin is basically heroin. It's China White. It's a refined derivative of opium, just like heroin. I'd say to my dad, "Holy shit, we're doing heroin! I've stopped…now you have to stop." We'd have long conversations and I'd plead with him, "Dad, there's this new thing and it works. It's called *not* using drugs and it's awesome." Just like when I was using drugs and someone at a party would say to me, "Hey, there's this new substance out, you have to try it, it's great." Well, here I was trying to explain to my dad, "There's this new thing, it's called *not* using drugs, and it's way better." I'd tell him how I used to be depressed and anxious all the time, had no control over my bowels, and had no ambition to work when I was using, but now that I was off drugs I was feeling completely different. He didn't want to believe me though. He was still in denial. He didn't want to stop using because that would mean he'd have to start dealing with the consequences from when he *was* using. That's the hardest part of giving up drugs. I saw my dad stuck in the same hole that I was in for so many years. I'd tell him that all he had to do was stop for a while and then he'd start to see that things would be okay. I'd say, "Just stop for even two hours. Because if you can stop for two hours, then you can stop for three." But he couldn't stop. By that point he was too far gone.

Finally, on January 5th, 2010, I had a conference call with my sisters to plan an intervention for my dad. I was about to leave for opie season in two days, and we decided that it was finally time to get professional help. We had exhausted all other options and this was our last chance. I called the top treatment facility in California and told the counselor that I'd like to schedule an intervention and reserve a room for my dad. He asked when I wanted to hold the intervention, to which I replied (and I'll never forget this), "Oh, three months should work. I have to go fishing in Alaska and then I'll come back and I can be a part of it." The counselor replied, "Why are you going to wait so long? Why not do it right now?" I thought about his question and agreed that it would be best to have the intervention before I left, even though it was short notice. The counselor continued, "Let me see what I can do and I'll call you back." But he never called back that day.

Later that evening, my girlfriend, Jenna, and I drove from Seattle to visit my dad in Anacortes. The drive takes about ninety minutes, and it was important to me that I saw my dad before I left for Alaska. We arrived at my parents' house at about 9 p.m. and I gave my dad a hug and said to him,

"You're a good dad. I don't want you to forget that." Jenna and I stayed for about an hour, and as we were beginning to drive away I said to her, "I've got to go back. I have to give my dad another hug. I've got to say goodbye to him again." We stopped in the middle of the street, about half a block away, and I went back inside to give my dad a final hug. I told him that I loved him and that he was the best dad anyone could hope for. Those were the last words I ever spoke to my dad.

The next day, January 6th, I was getting ready for my trip up north when I received a call from my sister, Megan, at about 8:30 p.m. She told me that my dad had been gone for several hours and she was getting worried. I assumed that he had left earlier in the afternoon to get Oxycontin, and I knew that roundtrip he's never gone for more than three hours. Because my dad never drove while under the influence, he was always in a hurry to get back home. Since he had been gone for over four hours, I knew something wasn't right. Even though I had an early flight to Alaska the next morning, Jenna and I drove to Anacortes as soon as I got off the phone with Megan. We arrived just after 10 p.m., and my sister, Johanna, explained what happened earlier that day. She said that while she was at my parents' house, she saw an unusual number appear on the home phone's caller ID at about 4 p.m. She picked up the phone and listened to the conversation. The caller was my dad's Oxycontin dealer, and my dad was planning to get more pills. Johanna was concerned, so she told my mom what she overheard. My mom became angry and argued with my dad, and at about 4:30 p.m., my dad left the house. Now, more than five hours later, my dad still hadn't returned home and my family was very concerned. We couldn't call his cell phone because he had lost it earlier that day, and not enough time had passed to file a missing person report. We were suspicious and fearful, but ultimately we hoped that my dad would arrive home safely any minute.

I only stayed at my parents' house for about an hour because I had to return home to pack for my trip to Alaska. I was scheduled to fly out of Seattle at 6 a.m. the next morning, and I had to stay focused on fishing. I had to do my best not to worry about my dad because I had to earn money for my family. If my dad was missing, then my family was going to need even more financial support.

The next morning I flew to Alaska as planned to fish opies on the *Northwestern*. It took everything

I had not to break down when I left Seattle. I relied on what I learned through my addiction support program, like stay in the moment, focus on my sobriety, and embrace life's experiences. But even more basic than that, I was just trying to hold it together until I received word that my dad was safe. This is why I find it insulting when people tell me that I need to "leave my personal life at home," and I need to worry about fishing when I'm on the boat. If there was ever a person who has done that to the best of his ability, it's me. It wasn't easy for me to leave my family when my dad was missing. It wasn't easy for me to say to my mom, "You call me when you want me to come home. Otherwise, it's going to be really hard for me to call you." I take strong offense when people tell me that I need to "leave my personal life at home" because I don't think anybody has done that better than me.

By the time I arrived in Dutch Harbor, it was already well known that my dad was missing. It was being covered by the Seattle news stations and it was public knowledge. There was nothing I could do except stay quiet until I knew more facts. I knew that anything I said on camera could easily be taken out of context. Who my dad was, and the great things he had done for his community could have been lost in anything that I said. For over thirty years my dad served his community as a high school counselor, and before that he protected his country as a Marine, but suddenly that was all being overshadowed by the two years he was addicted to painkillers. More than anything, I didn't want my dad to be remembered as a drug addict, so I refused to talk about him on camera.

I'm grateful that my uncle Nick was with me that season on the *Northwestern*. I confided in Nick while my dad was missing and I couldn't have made it through the season without him. I would tell Nick what I was feeling and I would break down and cry. He was always there for me and I wouldn't have cried around anybody else. You're not supposed to show weakness to other fishermen and you're definitely not supposed to cry in front of them. But because Nick was family, I knew that I could let my guard down.

Days went by and there was still no update on my dad. I was going through the motions of my job, but it was hard not to think about what might have happened to him. As scared and anxious as I felt, I thank God that I was never tempted to relapse. I had been clean for six months, and I was no longer looking for an excuse to get high. I had fought since the age of twenty, every day of my life, whether I was at sea or at home, to find a way not to drink and drug the way that I was. That's what people don't understand about me. I fought with *everything I had* not to use drugs. I had finally broken my addiction and I was going to be damned, I was going to die, before I was going to use again. And I was adamant about that. So I had no problem not using drugs while my dad was missing. There were no more excuses. I said to myself, "Okay, this is life. This is an experience and I need to embrace it. I'm going to face this sober. I'm not going through this as a weak man. I'm going through this all out and with my head up high." And that's exactly what I did.

I didn't know it at the time, but while my dad was missing, Sig had been calling my family every day to check in. He would call two or three times per day, which is what I should have been doing but wasn't strong enough to. Sig knew more about my father's case than I did and he tried not to worry me. Then, about two weeks into the season, a cameraman approached me on deck and said, "Jake, we need you to call your mom." I had no idea why I had to call home or what to expect. But

I went into the wheelhouse, called my mom, and the first words I heard were, "Jake, they found the truck, but they haven't found him yet." At that moment I knew I would never see my dad again. I felt numb as I played through the different scenarios in my head. Did somebody hurt him? Did he hurt himself? Did he have an accident? The only explanation that I was willing to accept was that my dad's truck had possibly run off the side of the road, and as he was trying to find help he slipped, hit his head, and then froze to death. That's what I was willing to accept at that moment. Nothing else made sense to me.

Even though my dad's truck was found, I still had more questions than answers. I didn't know where my dad was or what happened to him. So I did the only thing that I knew how to do; I fished. I continued to do my job on deck until February 9th, when Sig and I flew home to Seattle. The day we left was the same day that Phil Harris passed away, and the entire fleet was in mourning. I loved Phil like a second father and I think of Jake and Josh Harris as my brothers. Losing Phil almost hurt as much as losing my dad.

*(From left) Jake Anderson, Ryan Simpson, Jake Harris*

*Phil Harris and Jake Anderson*

When I arrived in Seattle, Jenna and I drove to Anacortes to be with my family. That same night, I received details about the ongoing police investigation. The lead detective told me that he still didn't know what happened to my dad. Apparently the police department searched for my dad after his truck was found, but for only six hours. To me, a six hour search was an insult. The detective told me they were doing "everything they could" to find him, yet they gave up on their search after only six hours. That was frustrating because we, as crab fishermen, search for up to forty, fifty, even sixty hours straight to find crab, but the police were only willing to search for six hours to find my dad. Six hours was a fucking joke. We search for six *months* with almost no sleep, no food, while we're shitting our pants in the freezing cold–almost killing ourselves–to find a crustacean, and they could only search six hours for one man. That was all the time they could devote to a person who was willing to serve his country as a Marine, and willing to serve his community as a high school counselor. When the detective told me that he had done "everything he could" to find my dad, he insulted me that day.

Later that night I saw the map of where my dad's truck was found. His white Ford Ranger was discovered abandoned off Darringer Park Road in a heavily wooded area of Darrington, Washington. The truck was locked and the keys were still inside. On the day of his disappearance, my dad had traveled to Sultan, Washington, about seventy miles south of Anacortes, to buy Oxycontin. Afterwards, my dad was supposedly on his way back to Anacortes when he disappeared. But there was an obvious problem. Darrington is in the mountains, and it's not directly between Sultan and Anacortes. In fact, his truck was discovered about thirty miles out of the way. My dad had apparently traveled from Sultan to Darrington using Highway 9, which is east of I-5, and right in the middle of the Cascade Mountain Range. Essentially, Darrington is part of a huge dense forest that's not heavily traveled. What most people don't know about the area is that it's a known spot where people go missing. There's bear, there's cougar, there's a lot of drugs that get run through there, and it's a popular spot to dump stolen cars. It's easy to hide something you're doing there if you wanted to.

Google

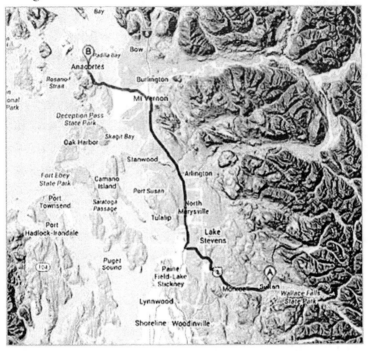

*Map from Sultan (A) to Anacortes (B)*

*Route from A to B: I-5 N*
*Distance: 70 miles*
*Drive Time: 1 hour 30 minutes*

Google

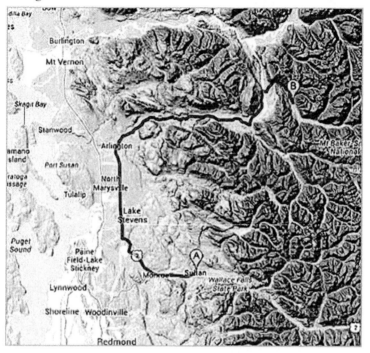

*Map from Sultan (A) to Darrington (B)*

*Route from A to B: WA-9 N*
*Distance: 60 miles*
*Drive Time: 1 hour 20 minutes*

Google

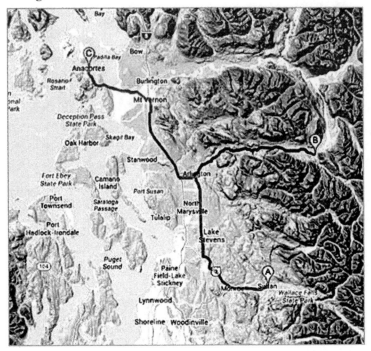

*Map from Sultan (A) to Darrington (B) to Anacortes (C)*

*Route from A to B: WA-9 N*
*Distance: 60 miles*
*Drive Time: 1 hour 20 minutes*

*Route from B to C: WA-530*
*Distance: 65 miles*
*Drive Time: 1 hour 30 minutes*

I had to see for myself where my dad's truck was found. I wanted to do my own search since the police had let my family down. Early the next morning, my friend Casey McManus picked me up in his truck and we drove to Darrington. Casey fished on the F/V *Billikin,* and we've been good friends for over five years. He brought four-wheelers in his trailer, and we also stopped by Sig's house to borrow his motorcycle. When we arrived in Darrington, we began to search for my dad. We planned to stay for three days and camp out until we found some sign that my dad was there. But as soon as we got out of Casey's truck, it became apparent that we were truly in the middle of nowhere. It's easy to understand how somebody could get lost if he was disoriented like my dad might have been. If he was tired and withdrawing from Oxycontin, it's possible that he might have made a wrong turn and never found his way back to the highway.

Near the end of our first day of searching we made our way down a small logging road that dead ended into a cul-de-sac. Where the road ended, a bike trail began. Since Casey was riding a four-wheeler and I was riding a motorcycle, we decided to take the trail. After a few hundred feet we came to a small hill, and beyond the hill was heavy forest that was too tight for the four-wheeler to pass through. Unable to go any farther, we decided to turn around. At that moment, I realized that we were in the exact location where my dad's truck was found. I could still see the truck's faint tire marks in the mud and I confirmed the location by GPS. Suddenly, everything came together and my opinion about what happened to my dad completely changed. It looked like somebody intentionally tried to bury his truck. There was no way my dad would have driven down a bike trail in a desolate forest to park his truck in the pitch black darkness. With this realization I started to become emotional.

Because this was the spot where my dad went missing, Casey and I set out food and water and we hung a cross. We knew he wouldn't be coming back, but it felt like the right thing to do. Then, we gave my dad a 21-gun salute. We used AR-15s and we were civilians, so it wasn't a real salute, but I made sure that my dad got the respect he deserved. After that, I couldn't search anymore. I was too beat up. After the long fishing season and then losing my dad and Phil Harris, I had nothing left in me. It was too much. The pain was too real.

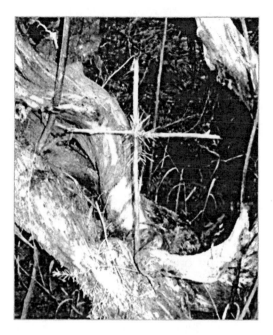

I wouldn't have been looking if we had stayed, I would have just been walking. So Casey and I decided to return to Seattle.

By the time we made it back to Casey's truck, it was nighttime. Being in that forest at night doesn't feel right. It's hard to describe, but it feels odd. As we were leaving Darrington we stopped at a remote gas station to ask the attendant if she had heard anything about my dad's case. I asked, "Do you know anything about that Keith Anderson person? We were up on Darringer Park Road looking for him. He's missing." I'll never forget her response, "What are you guys doing up there? Don't you know that people go missing up there all the time?" Her words were unsettling. We hadn't feared for our safety while we were in the woods because we brought AK-47s, AR-15s, pistols, and a riot shotgun. We had so many guns that we weren't scared of anything. But the gas station attendant was giving us a warning and it was unnerving.

The following day I talked to the lead detective again. I had read news reports online that said blood was found on the truck's key fob and on the windshield. I asked the detective if the reports were true, and he told me that only trace amounts of red paint were found, but not blood. I asked how he knew it was red paint, and he told me that although the department hadn't run a DNA swab on the sample, he was fairly sure that it was just paint. Knowing that it didn't make sense for my dad to carry paint in his truck, I asked the detective to test the sample for DNA. He initially refused, but after my family insisted, the sample was eventually tested and it was proven that the red substance was, in fact, my dad's blood. That was so frustrating because I had been begging the police to find my dad and they continued to tell me they were doing everything they could, but they didn't even bother to test the red substance found in his truck. The detective also gave up on the investigation into the man from Sultan who was the last known person to see my dad alive. His excuse was that he didn't want to interfere with a separate ongoing investigation.

My family did everything possible to find my dad when the police let us down. My mom even brought a medium to her house in order to find answers. I'm a skeptic and don't believe in the supernatural, but we were doing everything we could to find my dad so I was willing to try it. When the medium arrived at my mom's house, we all sat in a circle and she began doing readings. She took turns speaking to each of us, and she seemed to focus on me longer than the others. She acknowledged that she knew who I was from the TV show, so I assumed she had looked up information about me prior to arriving. I was naturally skeptical until she said to me, "So, tell me about your coin." Her statement caught me off guard. Earlier that morning, back in Seattle, I received a sobriety coin from my addiction support group. No one in the room knew what I had done that day, and I received the coin at a meeting I hadn't planned on attending. In fact, I hadn't told anyone that I received the coin because it was only important to me. So when the medium asked about my coin I was surprised. After she took turns reading each of us, she did a final reading for my dad. She told us that someone had harmed him, but she didn't know who or why. I'm still a skeptic, but the experience was interesting to say the least.

Weeks went by and there was still no progress being made in my dad's case. The police were starting to give up on my dad but the Anacortes community was not. The entire community came together and did so much for my family while my dad was missing. They conducted private searches, they kept my dad's reputation intact to the media, and they raised money for a reward through fundraisers. At one community fundraiser in Ballard, Washington, Jake and Josh Harris, Scott Hillstrand, Nick, Edgar, and Keith Colburn came out to support my family. My friends and the Anacortes community did a lot for my dad. They did more than me.

Although the community was conducting regular searches near the area where my dad's truck was found, I could never bring myself to go back to Darrington. The only other time I visited the site was with the TV show camera crew. My mom doesn't like me going to those woods alone, and I honor what she says. Besides, I know she's probably right. The logging roads are winding and dangerous, and they're completely surrounded by forest. There are many stories about people going missing in those woods, and the more time you spend there, the more you feel like you're not supposed to be there. In fact, while we were filming the TV segment, one of the cameramen had to take a leak but refused to get out of the car because he was too scared.

Just as we were about to give up hope that we'd ever find my dad, my mom was notified that his partial remains were discovered by a hiker in Darrington. It was July 2012, and two long years had passed since my dad disappeared. I was fishing on the *Northwestern* in Prince William Sound at the time, and my mom told me that only his tibia and part of his skull were recovered. Thoughts raced through my head, just like when she told me that his truck was found two years earlier. The first question I asked was, "Where did they find him?" The answer was like getting punched in the face. His bones were discovered just *one mile* from where his truck was found. One mile. The guilt of knowing that I was so close to finding him almost kills me. If I had been stronger and went back to look for my dad like I should have, I know I would have found him. My next question was, "Did they find his wallet?" The answer was no. There was no wallet, no clothes, and no valuables of any kind. Just partial bones.

Google

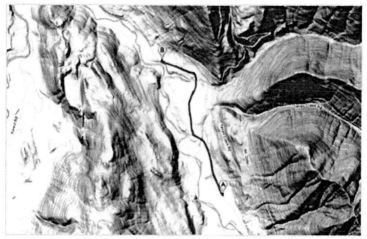

*Map from Truck (A) to Body (B)*
*Distance: <1 mile*

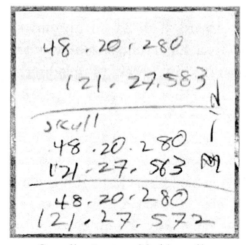

*Coordinates provided by police*

As devastating as it was to know that my dad would never be coming home, I was relieved that we found him. We were able to have a cremation service and finally lay him to rest. My family spread his ashes off the coast of Neah Bay, Washington, and we gave him the Viking-style burial at sea he always wanted. Up until the time my dad was found, I held a lot of jealousy towards Jake and Josh Harris. When my dad went missing, it was the same time that Phil passed away. When Jake and Josh spread Phil's ashes off the rail of the F/V *Cornelia Marie*, I had to pretend that I was burying my dad, too. Finally being able to lay my dad to rest brought peace to my family. In his honor we established the Dr. Keith Anderson Bootstrap Award. This is an annual scholarship presented to a high school senior who has overcome adversity in order to graduate. My dad would be proud that his legacy of helping others is continuing even after his death.

Looking back, I still don't know what happened to my dad. I don't know if his death was an accident, if he harmed himself, or if he was harmed by somebody else. I don't think I'll ever know the truth. The only way I get through my day is through forgiveness for the person who last saw

*Friends and family gathered to spread Keith's ashes*

*Celebrating Keith's life. (From left) Jake, Johanna,
Megan, Wendy, and Beth Anderson*

him, forgiveness for the police department, and forgiveness for my dad. I've given up on all the theories because it doesn't change the fact that my dad's gone. I don't think it's important to know what happened to him anymore. I've talked to many people who have had a missing person in their family and I've found they tend to lose their minds over all the theories. To be so consumed by it, there would be no way for me to find peace in my life. Worrying about my dad was almost too much for me to bear. I went as far as I could, but it wasn't very far.

It seems like things happened so perfectly the day my dad disappeared that we weren't meant to keep him here on earth. Between the intervention we were about to have and the fact that he lost his cell phone the same day he went missing, it started to become clear that we weren't going to hold him on earth another day. When I feel trapped by the guilt that I could have done more or that somebody may have harmed my dad, I recite the Lord's Prayer, *"Forgive us our trespasses, as we forgive those who trespass against us."* Continued forgiveness is healing. It's allowed me to keep my sobriety and live a normal life, even while all this chaos and turmoil is happening around me. Instead of giving up, doing drugs, and living in despair, I'm able to get out of bed each morning, do a job that I love, and live my life.

Everything that keeps me going today is to make my dad proud. When he went missing, I didn't have the choice to give in to depression and drugs. His death made me push harder to be a better man, and I hope he's proud of me. I'll always consider him to be the greatest dad and the smartest person I'll ever know. I never thought less of him because he couldn't fix the problems within himself. Nothing will ever change what I think about my dad.

# 5

# Fishing Saved My Life

Following the loss of my dad, fishing saved my life for the second time. The first time it saved me from addiction, and the second time it saved me from my own thoughts. When my dad went missing I needed something positive to focus my energy on. I fished for six to eight months out of the year, but my time spent at home was still difficult. I've seen other people deal with tragedies, and I've seen some of them get lost in their grief and never come back. I didn't want that to happen to me, so I decided to attend classes at the Crawford Nautical School in Seattle to distract me from my thoughts.

In 2010, I enrolled in the Able Bodied Seaman (AB) program at Crawford. Once I had my AB license, I'd be certified to perform all routine deck duties on inspected vessels, and it would help improve safety on board the *Northwestern*. Before classes began, the director of the school, Patsy Crawford, asked why I wanted to apply for an AB license when I could instead apply for a captain's license. I considered her question and replied, "No way...There's no way I'm going to apply for a captain's license." I wasn't very educated, I wasn't well read, and I didn't know if I'd be able to pull off an AB license, let alone a captain's license. I was also fishing in Alaska for over half the year and my limited time at home needed to be spent supporting my mom and sisters. But then I started to look at Patsy's offer as an opportunity. I learned through my addiction support group to embrace new experiences and to not go through life as a weak man. I also learned that I had to put straightening up my life *first* before everything else. So after reconsidering Patsy's offer, I accepted. I decided to apply for my Master 100-ton license and USCG Mate 1600-ton license.

If I successfully completed the coursework and passed the exams, I would be able to serve as the captain of a 100-ton inspected vessel and the mate of a 1600-ton inspected vessel. The only other licensed member of the *Northwestern* was Sig. He had the Master 1600-ton license, which I hoped to someday work up to through certification upgrades. What a lot of people don't know about the maritime industry is there's no basic credential required to work as a deckhand in the Bering Sea. Anyone can do it and there are very few safety regulations. That's what makes crabbing so dangerous. There's little training offered to deckhands and the boats themselves are small to begin with. A 28-foot by 127-foot vessel is defenseless against a sixty or seventy foot wave. Even a twenty foot

*Jake Anderson and Edgar Hansen*

swell can be dangerous. As of late, the Coast Guard has added more regulations as to what types of safety equipment are required on board, but most boats today still don't require life jackets or helmets on deck. The United States Occupational Safety and Health Administration (OSHA) is not a big part of the fishery either. I remember times when Edgar and I would climb the mast of the *Northwestern* to fix light casings when the wind was blowing fifty knots. There were no lanyards or safety ropes; we just used one arm to hold onto the mast and the other arm to fix the light. It took everything we had not to fall into the Bering Sea. Examples like that are what makes the fishing industry so dangerous and makes boat insurance so expensive. If I earned my captain's license it would help reduce the high cost of insurance, and it would put me into a long line of mariners patiently waiting to be skippers.

By the time I started attending classes at Crawford, I had already learned how to perform all of the deck duties on the *Northwestern*. I knew how to stack pots, run hydraulics, and operate the crane, and I was slowly learning how to operate the engine room. On the *Northwestern*, I never went into the engine room unless Edgar invited me. It was *his* engine room and having too many people working in such a small space could cause serious and dangerous problems. The saying *too many chiefs, not enough Indians* definitely holds true for the confined space of the engine room. But in the summer of 2010, when Edgar took the season off from salmon fishing, I was given sole responsibility of managing the *Northwestern's* engine room for the first time. I was responsible for everything that happened downstairs and on deck, and by the end of the summer I could do every job the boat had to offer. The only part of the *Northwestern* that I had yet to learn was the wheelhouse, and my classes at Crawford were preparing me for those duties as well.

To earn my Master 100-ton and USCG Mate 1600-ton fishing license, I had to attend lectures at Crawford and pass a series of exams. Because of my busy fishing schedule, it took me almost two years to pass the exams. There was also a lot of safety training required and I had to meet the prerequisite of having at least 1,080 days of service on a vessel. I finally completed the requirements in June of 2012 and I was given my Merchant Mariner Credential by the Coast Guard. I was a licensed captain.

To me, getting my captain's license meant a lot of things. It meant that I had come a long way from the time I was living on the streets in Anacortes. It meant that I was advancing in my career as a fisherman. But more than anything, it meant that I wasn't a scumbag anymore. Just a few years earlier I was behaving like a child. I didn't know how to handle difficult situations and I couldn't be trusted with a dollar. But I made the decision

within myself to improve, and with the help of my support group, my family, and my girlfriend, Jenna, I turned into a person who was trusted by the Department of Homeland Security to be the captain of a vessel. For the first time I didn't regret being a former alcoholic and drug addict. Because if I wasn't an alcoholic and addict who gained sobriety and the insight that came with it, I would

*F/V Northwestern*

have never been able to survive the loss of my dad and then persevere to earn my captain's license. My past mistakes had led me to some place positive and allowed me to put everything in perspective.

Once I had my Master 100-ton license, I started looking into what it would take to earn my 200-ton license. The upgrade would allow me to be the captain of a larger inspected vessel, and it would bring me one step closer to achieving my ultimate goal of earning my Master 1600-ton license. But the only way to upgrade to a higher level is through logging sea time as a captain. To be eligible for the Master 200-ton license, I would have to log at least 180 days in the wheelhouse. That meant Sig would have to sign off on my days as I earned them, and I'd have to be patient to earn time at the helm. I was willing to wait for my opportunity on the *Northwestern*, but then in the fall of 2012 I received an unexpected offer from Aleutian Spray Fisheries. They asked me to train to be the skipper of their renowned crab boat, the F/V *Kiska Sea*.

# The Kiska Sea

By the start of the 2012 king crab season, word had spread around the fleet that I was looking to move into the wheelhouse. I had no intention of leaving the *Northwestern*, but I began receiving job offers from other crab boats. The most attractive offer came from Mike Wilson, the captain of the *Kiska Sea*. Mike approached me in Dutch Harbor just before the start of the king crab season. He introduced himself and said, "My company wanted me to come talk to you. They wanted me to ask if you're interested in possibly running the *Kiska Sea* in the future." He continued, "I don't know what your plans are, but I think the company wants me to retire." Of course I was interested in Mike's offer. The *Kiska Sea* was a well-respected crab boat with an impressive reputation. I thanked Mike for his offer and that was the end of our brief conversation.

A few weeks later I received a phone call from Chris Swasand, the President of Aleutian Spray Fisheries. They were the highly regarded Seattle-based corporation that owned and operated the *Kiska Sea*. Chris was in charge of hiring captains for each boat in the fleet, and the captains then hired their own crew. During a short phone conversation with Chris, he reiterated Mike's offer and asked if I'd like to be the next skipper of the *Kiska Sea*.

Being offered the chance to run my own boat was too good to pass up. Even though I loved working on the deck of the *Northwestern*, I felt like I had to take the opportunity to move forward with my career. Right or wrong, I knew that I had to leave the *Northwestern* to join the *Kiska Sea*. I dreaded having to tell Sig that I wasn't coming back. I remembered back to the day when he gave me his *Northwestern* jacket, and how it meant that I was never supposed to leave. But I *was* leaving, and I didn't know how Sig would react.

When I sat down to tell him, Edgar, Matt, and Nick, I tried to be honest about my intentions and grateful for what they had taught me. I told them that I loved them like brothers, but I would not be returning to the *Northwestern*. As soon as the words left my mouth, the reality of my decision set in. But at the same time I also felt relieved. I was proud that I had made the decision on my own and that I wasn't influenced by anybody else. I didn't have any regrets as I left Sig's house that day.

When I accepted the job on the *Kiska Sea* for the 2013 opie season, TV cameras weren't planning to follow me on board. I didn't care. I was finally given the opportunity to run a crab boat, and even if it was for less money or less fame, it didn't matter. Being captain was my dream and it was the reason that I attended nautical school for over two years. After signing my contract with the *Kiska Sea*, I told the boat owner, the captain, and the crew, that cameras *would not* be following me. I made it clear that I was there to fish and to learn the operation. I was excited for the new opportunity and I didn't want any distractions.

But just before the season began, I received a phone call from the TV show producers. Their plans changed and they asked if they could follow me on the *Kiska Sea*. Honestly, I had my reservations about continuing with the show. I wanted the season to be only about fishing and I didn't want any interruptions. But as someone who was aspiring to be captain, I knew that it was my job to earn money for the company. Whether the money came from crab, cameras, packing salmon, or selling apples off the back of the boat, a good captain does what's needed to turn a profit. If I was going to deny the company money, then I would not be acting like a true captain. So I contacted Chris Swasand, told him about the offer, and he agreed to allow the cameras on board. It would mean a little bit of money for the *Kiska Sea* and a marketing opportunity for Aleutian Spray Fisheries. So I accepted the offer, and with the cameras on board we started the season.

I learned how to operate the deck during the first few days of the season. I understood how the deck was configured and the roles and responsibilities of each deckhand. My next step was to learn the engine room, but that's when my progress abruptly stopped. Mike Wilson was already training another crew member in the engine room and there started to be a conflict of interest. Part of

*F/V Kiska Sea*

the crew began to resent me because they thought
I was invading their territory. But I was just doing what the company hired me to do, which was
to learn how to run the boat. When the current
engineer started to see me as a threat, I began to
have huge crew member issues.

Two crew members in particular absolutely did
not like me. They didn't like the fact that I was on
television, they didn't like the fact that Chris
hired me directly, and they didn't like the fact that
I was supposedly moving into the wheelhouse. If
Mike were to promote me above these two crew
members, they would have either quit or tried to

make my life miserable, which was exactly what they did.

First, it should be said that I did make a few good friends on deck. There were some crew members who wanted to see me move into the wheelhouse and we got along great. But the two crew members who mistreated me were well-respected on the boat. The problems started as soon as we left Dutch Harbor. I caught them going through my locker, digging through my paychecks, and reading my private contracts. From the moment I woke up in the morning I was subjected to heavy ridicule. If I worked hard on deck, I got made fun of for working *too hard*. If I only did the work that was necessary, I got hazed for that. If I made a trivial mistake on deck, they used it to demonstrate to the crew that I wasn't prepared to run the boat. They exploited everything I did that they perceived to be a mistake, even down to how I put silverware in the dish drainer. From day one, they were determined to make me quit by trying to show that I was incompetent, which wasn't true. The *Kiska Sea* prides itself on being a professional operation, but I saw very little professionalism from those two crew members.

By the end of the season, one of the friends I had made on deck, Casey Bays, was so disgusted by the way one crew member had treated me that he asked Mike Wilson, "When we deliver our last crab, can I go onto the dock and beat the shit out of him?" Mike didn't give his approval, but Casey subscribed to the old mariner rule *whatever happens on the dock, stays on the dock*. So after the last crab was offloaded and we were about to return the boat to the shipyard, Casey ran up to this crew member on the dock and knocked him out cold.

*Casey Bays*

In the beginning, when I told Sig that I would be leaving the *Northwestern* to join the *Kiska Sea*, he wouldn't give me his blessing. He had fished for long enough to know what was going to happen to me aboard the *Kiska Sea*. He warned me, but I didn't want to believe him. I thought Sig was holding me back, but he was really showing genuine concern. He didn't want to see me fail. He knew that if I joined a boat like the *Kiska Sea*, where there was a lot of pride involved, and then expected the captain to give up control to somebody with little experience, it wasn't going to end well. Sig warned me that the crew members were not going to let me run the boat, either. Pretty much everything that Sig said would happen, did happen. But I needed to learn the lesson on my own.

In the end, I understood why some crew members treated me the way they did, but it didn't mean I had to tolerate it. They had been deckhands on the *Kiska Sea* for a long time, so in their eyes they had more experience than me. But in my eyes, I still deserved their respect. I had been in charge of an engine room, I had navigated the *Northwestern* from Alaska to Seattle through the Ballard Locks, I had docked a boat, and I had dealt with the Coast Guard. I've had those responsibilities whereas the deckhands on the *Kiska Sea* have not. They perceived my adjustment to learning a new boat and a new fishing operation as a lack of experience. In reality, I just hadn't experienced their specific way of doing things.

As much as I regretted being mistreated and disrespected on camera, I didn't regret my decision to be filmed on the *Kiska Sea*. At the end of the day, I knew that I was making money for Aleutian Spray Fisheries. That was all that mattered to me. The two crew members who tried to make my life miserable never understood that I was generating revenue and helping the company. They thought they were the best in the Bering Sea and I was an amateur, but in reality they were doing replaceable jobs while I was making a contribution to the company's bottom line. Their lack of basic business knowledge, and the fact that they were oblivious to how the fishery works in general, made it a lot easier to tolerate their heckling. They had fished with the *Kiska Sea* for years, but they were both acting like greenhorns so their ridicule didn't bother me.

Although Mike Wilson didn't give me the training that I felt I was promised, he treated me with respect and he was an excellent fisherman. He knew that I wanted to be captain, which meant that I needed him to teach me about the boat's insurance, who the co-ops were, what State Department paperwork needed to be filed, and how to complete the federal logbook. He also knew that I needed more time at the helm to get adequate boat handling experience. I was used to a single screw engine and the *Kiska Sea* was a twin screw. A different set of handling skills were required and I needed time to learn the maneuvers. But Mike was reluctant to let me move forward and I understood his position. We had a lot of crab to catch and promoting me would have created conflict with certain crew members. I recognized that it was ultimately his decision as to who was going to run the *Kiska Sea*, and if he felt that I wasn't the right person for the job, I wasn't going to argue with him. I was just going to fulfill my contract like a good fisherman and then leave, which is exactly what I did.

I fished with the *Kiska Sea* from December 28th, 2012 to June 12th, 2013. When I returned to Seattle I sat down with Chris Swasand and told him that I would not be returning the following season. I explained, "The *Kiska Sea* is not going to work for me. The skipper's never going to quit and the guys absolutely don't like who I am because I'm on television. They're not going to follow me if I move into the wheelhouse." Chris explained the situation as he saw it, but it didn't change my mind. From his explanation, the words that he spoke to Mike Wilson were different than the words Mike spoke to me. When I told Chris that Mike had approached me before the season began and asked me to take over the boat for him, Chris denied telling Mike that I would be running the *Kiska Sea*. According to Chris, he told Mike that I would be running *a boat* with the company, but he never told Mike *which boat*. That's when I realized this was all my fault because I should have communicated better with Mike and Chris. I should have said to both of them, "So, will I be captain in two years...three years...what am I looking at? What's my five year plan with the company?" When Mike asked if I wanted to run the *Kiska Sea*, and then Chris hired me with the intention that I'd be captain, I believed that great things were going to happen. It was easy for me to get lost in the dream of running my own boat within the next few years. I should have managed my expectations better and specified in my contract exactly why I was there and what I was hired to do. I don't blame

Chris or Mike for how things turned out. If it was anybody's fault, it was mine. I made the decision to join the *Kiska Sea* and I didn't cross my T's and dot my I's before the season began.

Today, I hold no animosity towards Chris or Mike. Chris was honest with me at the end of the season and told me that my chances of running a boat in the near future were slim. He did an excellent job under the circumstances and I'm glad to consider him my friend today. As for Mike, he was an excellent fisherman and I respect him as a captain. He deserves the trust and respect of his crew, and any crabber in the Bering Sea should consider himself lucky to work for Mike and Aleutian Spray Fisheries. But at the same time, I can't help but question why I was hired in the first place. Was I hired based on my skills and reputation? Or because I might come with a TV contract? From now on, if a company tries to hire me and throws around phrases like "you'll be captain" and "you'll run the boat," they may be approached for a TV contract. I'll have to be careful whether I'm being hired to actually be the skipper or if I'm being hired to look like a skipper on TV.

At the end of the day, I wasn't responsible for anything on the *Kiska Sea*. My sole intention for leaving the *Northwestern* was to have more responsibility and more opportunity. But after six months on the *Kiska Sea* I actually had less responsibility. I had moved backwards. If I would have stayed, I would have been working as a deckhand. And if I was going to work on deck, even if it was for one more day, it was going to be for Sig Hansen. It wasn't going to be for anybody else.

# Going Home

After I left the *Kiska Sea*, I was adamant that I was done fishing in the Bering Sea. I thought my reputation was destroyed. I assumed that everybody in the fleet—my peers, the captains and boat owners—were going to believe what the *Kiska Sea* deckhands said about me on camera. I figured they'd assume I wasn't the guy that Sig and Edgar made me out to be. I was so lost after fishing on the *Kiska Sea* and I really hated who I was. I didn't like being considered a "reality star" anymore and I wanted to be done with the fishery. My plan was to leave Seattle and get a job on a Crowley tug boat out of Tampa, Florida. In fact, I was in the middle of gathering my paperwork to go tugging when I started receiving job offers from other crab boats. But I was still determined to leave the fishery because I knew that my chances of becoming a skipper were slim.

What finally changed my mind was a conversation that I had with Sig and Edgar in the summer of 2013. They were in downtown Seattle on business and we met under the Magnolia Bridge to discuss the upcoming king crab season. After a short greeting, Sig asked, "So, are you in or are you out?" I had already given that question a lot of thought. I replied, "I really want to come back home." The three of us talked and we decided that

*Sig Hansen*

*Jake Anderson and Sig Hansen*

it would be best for me, and best for the boat, if I returned for another season. I had fished with the *Northwestern* for so many years that I knew the operation inside and out, and coming back would save Sig and Edgar from having to train another greenhorn. At the end of our conversation Sig agreed to give me one last chance.

What made me want to return to the *Northwestern*, more than anything else, was that I wanted to fish king crab with Sig one more time. I realized that the *Northwestern*, my uncle Nick, Matt Bradley, and the Hansens, were a big part of my life. I felt beat up after my season on the *Kiska*

*Sea* and I wanted to reconnect with my brothers to remember what real fishing felt like.

When I returned to the *Northwestern* in October 2013, nothing had changed except for me. For the six months that I had fished on the *Kiska Sea* I did nothing but miss the *Northwestern*. I didn't want to talk about what I had been through, I was just happy to be home. But on my first day back, Sig gave me a wakeup call. He said to me, "Because you're family, we're giving you one more chance. Then you're on your own." Sig brought up

*(From left) Norman Hansen, Edgar Hansen,*
*Ben Shearin, Nick Mavar, Matt Bradley*

*(From left) Edgar Hansen, Ben Shearin,
Nick Mavar, Matt Bradley*

a good point. We *were* family. I missed Nick, Matt, Norman, Edgar, and Sig while I was away and I was proud to fish by their side again. I had other job opportunities after leaving the *Kiska Sea*, and I would have survived without returning to the *Northwestern*, but I wanted to come back. I missed the old Norwegian traditions like biting the head off a herring to start the season and throwing a flaming hook to finish the season. I was grateful to be home, and the 2013 king crab season on the *Northwestern* was the most satisfying season I've ever had.

*Edgar Hansen*

After I returned to the *Northwestern* I realized why my experiences on the *Kiska Sea* were so different. The answer comes down to one word: family. On the *Northwestern* we all hazed each other, but it was more like the hazing between brothers. On the *Kiska Sea* the hazing was directed *at me* personally. On the *Kiska Sea* they didn't want me to be there, but on the *Northwestern* they didn't want me to leave. Working on the *Kiska Sea* was like going to a job, but returning to the *Northwestern* was like going home.

# 8

# Waimea Canyon

If fishing saved my life twice, then my wife, Jenna, saved my life the third time. I met Jenna in July of 2008. I had just returned from salmon fishing in Bristol Bay, and the crew of the *Northwestern* was doing maintenance work at the Pacific Fishermen Shipyard in Seattle. It was the same week as the annual Seafair Festival on Lake Washington, which is a huge event that attracts thousands of people to the area. Sig was Grand Marshal of the Seafair Parade, and hundreds of fans had gathered outside the shipyard gate to take pictures of the *Northwestern*. No one was allowed inside the shipyard except for crew members, but after the crowd had gathered for a few hours a fan managed to get inside the gate so he could get a closer look at the boat. As soon as the gate opened, hundreds of fans pushed through and the shipyard became flooded with people. Because it's a potential liability nightmare for the *North-western*, we had to quickly usher everybody back out. But we still wanted to be polite, so we posed for a few pictures and signed autographs as we showed people to the exit.

It took about half an hour, but we finally managed to get everybody out of the shipyard. Just as I was escorting the last fan out, a group of two young women and two girls stopped me to ask for an autograph. We talked for a few minutes, I gave them my autograph, and then the youngest girl asked for a tour of the boat. I knew I shouldn't bring them into the shipyard but I wanted to be polite, so I agreed to give the family a quick tour. We walked down the dock, made our way onto the *Northwestern*, and I showed them around for about ten minutes. Afterwards, I walked them back to the exit gate, we took a few more pictures, and I went on my way.

Hours later I found out that one of the young girls on the tour had apparently convinced her aunt to leave me her phone number. Since I had already left the shipyard, she gave her number to Matt Bradley to pass along to me later. The aunt, who was a cute girl in her early twenties, turned out to be my future wife, Jenna, and the young girl is now my niece, Sierra.

When I returned to the shipyard later that night, Matt told me what happened. I remembered Jenna from our tour and I thought she was really cute. But I remember thinking that maybe I shouldn't call her. All my life, I've always wanted and loved girls. If alcohol was the worst drug in my life, then girls were a close second. They were the cause of all my problems, all my suffering, and all my joy. But after the season I had just had on the *Northwestern*, I was feeling confident. I finally had a great job, money in the bank, and I was feeling good about myself. So I decided to call her. The first time I tried calling, Jenna didn't answer. "Time to move on," I thought. But I decided to try again. Still no answer, and I didn't leave a message. I had a blocked phone number back then–I thought I was much cooler than I really was–so Jenna couldn't have called me back even if she wanted to. At least that's what I kept telling myself. The next day, I figured I would give it one

*Meeting Jenna for the first time*

last try. If Jenna didn't answer this time, I was going to lose the number. But the third time I called, Jenna answered and we talked for hours. We continued to talk every day for the next two weeks and we became really good friends. She was the first girl that I ever became friends with before we started dating.

Towards the end of our two week phone relationship, I had to fly to Rhode Island to do a promotional event for the clothing company *Helly Hansen.* I still hadn't seen Jenna except for the few minutes we spent together during the boat tour, but I knew I was falling for her. When I arrived back in Seattle, she was waiting for me at the airport. I knew right then I had found the person I wanted to spend my life with.

My wife is a beautiful person, but the funny thing is, on the day that we met she was wearing an old ragged sweatshirt, beat up shoes, and an old pair of jeans. I'm a superficial person. I admit that. I like nice things and I'm adamant about dressing well when I'm at home or on the boat. So when I saw Jenna for the first time, she was more or less just hanging out and not trying to impress anybody. I think that's what I liked most about her when we first met. She was just being herself.

From the moment I met Jenna, my life started to change. I was living on the *Northwestern* at the time to try to stay out of trouble. I still wasn't living right, but Jenna was making me a better person. She helped me recover from the loss of my sister in early 2009, and then on July 20th, 2009, she helped me give up drugs for the last time. The next day, July 21st, Jenna and I rented our first apartment together in Seattle. It was a small nine

hundred square foot, one-bedroom apartment on 88th and Stone Avenue, and we were happy there. Once we started living together my life rapidly changed. I moved in with Jenna in July, by August we were settled in and planning our future, and a few months later I was enrolled at the Crawford Nautical School planning to get my captain's license.

The beginning of our relationship was difficult because I was fishing in Alaska for six to eight months out of the year. Jenna worried for my safety and I know that it was hard on her. But the more she got to know the guys on the *Northwestern*, the more she felt at ease. She liked knowing that I was with my brothers. She knew they'd take good care of me and we'd keep each other safe. Even today, she feels that if something were to happen to me while I was on the *Northwestern* it would be due to fate and not because of a careless accident.

It was clear to me and my family that the more time I spent with Jenna, the better person I became. But it wasn't until June of 2011 that I knew I could never love anybody else. That month I was attending a promotional event in Florida for the company *West Marine*, when a beautiful girl approached me and we started talking. She recognized me from TV and asked if she could give me her phone number. I don't know why, but I said, "Okay," and I took down her number. In my mind, I was just trying to be nice and I had no intention of calling her. But I felt horrible. Right away, I felt guilty. I should have been honest with her and said, "No, I can't take down your number. I'm not available." But I was too uncomfortable to say that and I made the wrong choice. As soon as I felt guilty about writing down her number, I realized something—that no matter how beautiful the girl was or how tempted I might be, I could never be with anybody else. That's when I knew how much

I loved Jenna, and that's when I decided to propose to her.

My trip to Florida was in June, and by July I was shopping for Jenna's engagement ring. I asked my mom and my sister, Beth, to help me find the perfect ring. Beth and I are a lot alike. We both love beautiful things, so I knew she would be the best source to help me buy something for the most beautiful person in my life. They drove down to Seattle and helped me choose a ring that Jenna would love. I was ready to propose, but first I wanted to ask for her parents' permission. I thought I might have a problem getting permission from Jenna's dad, Judo, since we had spent very little time together. But Judo was a fisherman so we had an instant connection. When I called him, I said, "Judo, I'd like to marry your daughter, but I need your permission before I can ask her." He replied, "Well, are you going to take care of her for the rest of your life?" I told him that I would and he said, "Alright, then you have my permission." It was a simple conversation and I was relieved when it was over. Now I only had to ask Jenna's mom, Cindy, which I thought would be easy. Cindy is very outgoing and we had spent a lot of time together over the past two years, so I didn't think anything could go wrong.

I tried calling Cindy a few times but I was having trouble reaching her. I started to get worried because I had planned to propose to Jenna during her family reunion in Kauai, which was just a few days away. I knew that her mom would be there, but I wanted to get her blessing before we left Seattle. After a few more failed attempts, I finally reached Cindy. She was teaching choir practice at the time and I could hear women singing in the background. It was hard for me to hear her, but I said, "Cindy, this is Jake...I'd like to propose to Jenna, but I need your blessing and permission." I thought Cindy was going to jump for joy because she and Jenna were so close and we'd spent so much time together. But not only *didn't* she jump for joy, but I got a long lecture about what I had to do in order to be a good husband for her daughter. It was really sweet for Cindy to do that because it showed how much she loved Jenna, but it was not a fun phone call. At one point during the conversation I remembered thinking, *She might actually tell me that I can't marry Jenna!* In the end, Cindy gave me her permission, but she set a few things straight first. She knew me a little better than

Judo did. She knew my history with addiction and certain mistakes I had made in the past. She let me know that I wasn't in the clear for anything I had done wrong, and my checkered past wasn't going to be erased by the good things I was now doing. She made me understand the responsibility I was taking on by asking Jenna to marry me. Before talking to Cindy I didn't fully understand what it meant to ask for her daughter's hand in marriage, but afterwards I did.

A few days later, Jenna's entire family flew to the reunion in Kauai. There were twenty-two of us, and Jenna's mom rented three huge houses for the week. I was nervous at the beginning of the trip because Jenna's family knew that I was planning to propose and I wanted everything to go right. I also had an expensive ring in my pocket that I was sure I was going to lose. I think Jenna and I both knew we would eventually get married, but from what I could tell she had no idea that I was going to propose in just a few days.

The day I planned to propose was the same day as the reunion party. The party was at night, so my plan was to take Jenna to Waimea Canyon at sunset and ask her to marry me. I wanted to propose at Waimea Canyon because it was a place we had been to before, and it was a place we both loved. The day didn't get off to a good start though. In fact, Jenna and I began arguing from the moment we woke up. Jenna wanted to go shopping for the party that evening, and I, of course, wanted to go to Waimea Canyon. I kept begging her to go to the canyon and she didn't understand why I was being so stubborn. She'd say, "Jake...What's wrong with you! I need to go shopping. Our family is having a big party tonight and this is important to me. This is why we're here!" The day wasn't going well, but I was determined to propose before the party. I kept pestering her until she eventually gave in and agreed to go to the canyon. On the way, the only thought running through my head was, "Oh God, this is gonna be horrible..." When we arrived, I set up my camera when Jenna turned away so that it was facing out over the canyon. I thought, "Please God, let this be recording," because I knew Jenna would want to watch the proposal later–assuming she said yes.

*Waimea Canyon*

I waited until the sun started to set behind the canyon and I got on my knee. As soon as I started to propose, I broke down and cried. Ever since my dad went missing I had not been able to cry, but I think the joy of the moment overcame me. It was almost like I knew this was always meant to happen, and the gravity of the moment caught up with me. After I pulled myself together, I finally asked Jenna to marry me.

She accepted.

*Reenacting proposal at family reunion "talent show"*

We were engaged in September of 2011 and we married in May of 2012. Jenna, her mom, and sisters, Dejah and Callie, did most of the wedding planning. My mom and sisters helped with my side while I was fishing in Alaska, and I took care of small things like renting a tux and making sure my friends and family were on the guest list. That season we fought horrible ice in the Bering Sea. Each trip seemed to drag on for longer than usual and I was only home for about five days between January and May. In fact, I barely made it back to Seattle in time for the wedding. Sig, Edgar, and

Casey McManus were all part of my wedding party, and we were each fishing in Alaska until three days before the wedding. We arrived home on Wednesday, May 9th, and the wedding was Saturday, May 12th.

Casey McManus threw my bachelor party together with just a day's notice. We had such a tight window between when we returned home and when I was getting married, but Casey did an unbelievable job. He rented a huge party bus and we went indoor skydiving and go-kart racing. A lot of my friends were able to attend, including Matt Bradley, and Johnathan and Scott Hillstrand. Toward the end of the night, we decided to go to a strip club in downtown Seattle. When we arrived, Casey bought everybody lap dances and we were having a great time, but Johnathan Hillstrand was getting furious. He absolutely did not like me getting a lap dance from anyone but my wife. He didn't want me to be there and he wasn't trying to hide it. He stayed for only a few minutes before he went back out to the bus to have another drink. About five minutes later, my friend, Brady, ran over to me and said, "The bus driver is kicking us out! He's saying we have to leave. We have to go right now!" None of us knew why we were being forced to leave. We had just gotten to the club, Casey had spent hundreds of dollars on drinks and lap dances, and now we were being kicked out. After Casey paid the tab, we ran outside to get back on the bus. Meanwhile, we saw Johnathan sliding into a taxi just as it was leaving. After our bus pulled away from the strip club, Casey asked the bus driver, "Hey Paul, why did we have to leave? I rented this bus until 6 a.m. and it's only midnight. So why did you kick us out?" We were about six or seven blocks from the strip club when Paul replied, "What? I didn't kick anybody out, it was the guy in the USA jacket! He said you all had to leave!" Johnathan had kicked us all out of the strip club because he didn't want to see me around strippers or alcohol. I still give Johnathan a hard time about it today. He went all "captain" on me and I wasn't even working for him!

*No one has been a better friend to me than Johnathan Hillstrand. I couldn't have recovered from the loss of my dad without him. He called me almost every day while my dad was missing and he always managed to take my mind off my problems for at least a few hours. He would call me out of the blue and say, "Hey, do you want to go to the go-karts?" Or he'd offer to take me with him and Scott to the NASCAR races. If we were both in Florida, he would drive for hours just so we could hang out. When I joined the Kiska Sea, I talked to him almost every day and gave him a play-by-play of what I was going through. I don't think TV viewers understand what kind of person Johnathan is. He's rough and tough, he's a businessman, he's a Bering Sea fisherman, but at the end of the day he's a family man who always takes care of his community and his friends. Johnathan has become more than a friend to me. He's become a family member.*

My bachelor party was on Thursday, and two days later Jenna and I were married. Jenna spent so much time planning every detail of our wedding, and the day turned out as perfect as we had hoped. We were married at the Woodmark Hotel on Lake Washington and we had about two hundred guests. Sig was the officiant, and having him marry us was one of the highlights of our wedding. Originally, either Jenna's mom, Cindy, or my uncle, Chris Anderson, were going to perform the ceremony. But one night, a few months before the wedding, Jenna and I were at Sig's house and the three of us started joking that Sig should marry us since he's our "captain." We were joking at the time, but then in all seriousness Sig asked if we were really considering it. The more we thought about it, the more it made perfect sense. Jenna is spiritual whereas I'm religious. She wanted a fun wedding and I wanted a religious wedding. Sig is religious and he knows how to have fun, so we decided to go for it. Sig went online to get his ordination and he couldn't have done a better job performing our ceremony.

I Jake Anderson
Take you Jenna Patterson
To Be my wife, my lover,
my Best Friend, The mother
of my Soon To Be children,
To Be patient when own
Kids piss me off, And To
Accept me when I piss
you off. To protect you
with my life, To give
everything I am I will Be
Faithful until The end. Jenna
you have been The best
Thing That ever happened To
me, and I promise I will
demk more water and The
water I do drink will NOT
Consist of The Ice in my
Quad Tall mocha! I love
you    Jake Andersons
vows

My best man was Casey Rigney. We had both come a long way since skateboarding together in Anacortes. His pro skateboard came out just a few months earlier and he was recently named one of the most underrated skateboarders by *Transworld Magazine*. He's still sponsored by *Arcade Skateboards* and he's a featured skater in the Cirque du Soleil show *Wintuk*. We've remained close over the years and he's never stopped looking out for me. In fact, it was Casey's skateboarding connections that allowed me to get *my* first skateboarding sponsor, *DVS Shoes*, in 2009. Casey put me in touch with a well-known skateboarding video producer, Tim Dowling, who was trying to get a job filming on a Bering Sea crab boat. Tim asked if I could help him, and I agreed, but only if he showed my old skateboarding footage to the executives at DVS. A few days later I got a call from the Vice President of DVS, Tim Gavin, and he agreed to sponsor me and let me design my own custom skate shoe. With Casey's help, we both became sponsored skateboarders and achieved our high school dreams.

*Jake Anderson and Casey Rigney*

*Casey McManus and Casey Rigney*

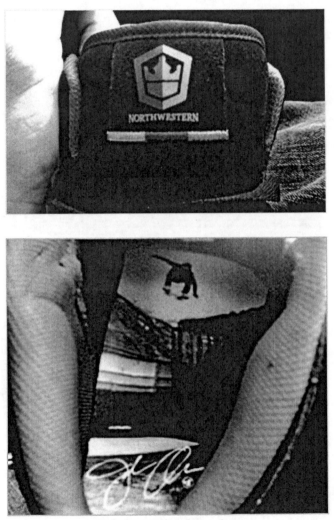

*Jake's custom skate shoe*

*DVS photo shoot*

At our wedding reception, we had two different cakes. One was a traditional wedding cake and the other was a Norwegian cake, called a *Kransekake*. The cake was layered with different sized rings, with each ring getting smaller towards the top of the cake. The Norwegian tradition is for the bride and groom to be blindfolded and then cut into the cake together. However deep they cut into the cake represents how many children they're going to have. So, as Jenna and I were blindfolded and holding the cake knife, our guests lifted up the Kransekake, making us cut deeper into the cake. There  were eight rings above our slice, which means we're supposed to have eight children. Jenna and I would like to start a family soon, but we both agree that eight children is a few too many. We'd love to have a boy and a girl. Although if we had a boy, I'd veer him away from the lifestyle of a fisherman. It's an honorable job, but being a fisherman is a hard life. You're never home with your family, there's usually a lot of alcohol involved, and the injury rate is one hundred percent. But if we're lucky enough to have children, we'll support anything they choose to do.

*(Back row, from left) Casey McManus, Casey Rigney,*
*Tony Avellino, Edgar Hansen (Front row, from left)*
*Jake Anderson, Silas Anderson*

The morning after our wedding, Sunday at 6 a.m., I had to fly back to Alaska to finish opie season. It's always hard to leave Jenna, and she's had to sacrifice a lot during our relationship. Being married to a fisherman, she's often by herself. I'm in Alaska for over half the year, and during my downtime I'm often traveling to promote the *Northwestern*. Even Jenna's life becomes exhausting because of my life. When I do come home and we finally have time to spend together, we're very boring people. We lead uninteresting lives and we like it that way. Jenna's also very focused on her career. She's a social worker and addiction counselor, and she's getting her graduate degree at the University of Washington. The funny thing is, for as gifted as Jenna is as a social worker, she cannot, for the life of her, help me. We sit and argue about the most ridiculous crap, but that's what I love about her. She never tries to change me. I think it's because she knows I'm a lost cause.

***

The best part of being on a popular TV show, for both of us, is the charity work we get to do and the people we get to help. Sig was the one who taught me how to use the show to help the community. The exposure has given us the opportunity to make a small difference in the causes we care most about. For Jenna and me, that's Seattle Children's Hospital, Make-A-Wish Foundation®, and the Fred Hutchinson Cancer Research Center. I keep thinking back to all the people in the Anacortes community who helped my family when my dad was missing. I always wanted to repay them, and the opportunities provided through the show have given me the chance to do that. I've been fortunate to participate in three wishes through Make-A-Wish, and each one has been life changing.

The first wish I participated in also involved Sig and the *Northwestern* crew. It was in August of 2008, just a few weeks after I met Jenna. I had been fishing on the *Northwestern* for a few years, and the crew had the opportunity to fulfill a wish for a ten year-old bone cancer survivor named Gary. His wish was simple; he wanted to go crab fishing on the *Northwestern*. Since we couldn't fly Gary to Dutch Harbor, we did the next best thing. We took him through the Ballard Locks to Puget Sound, dropped a few crab pots, and appointed Gary "Captain of the *Northwestern*" for the day. We also had the Department of Fish and Game come out to perform a surprise "inspection" of the boat. They arrived with flashing lights and megaphones, and they insisted on boarding our ship. They came into the wheelhouse and demanded to know who the captain was. Sig replied, "Don't look at me...The captain's right there, it's Gary!" With a huge smile, Gary kept yelling, "I'm not the captain! I'm not the captain!" as he pointed back to Sig. That day Gary experienced what it was like to

be a crabber, without the fifty foot waves or sub-
zero temperatures.

The second wish I took part in came a few years
later, in April of 2010. It involved Edgar, myself,
and a thirteen year-old boy named Erik. Erik's
wish was to become a superhero. My friend, Jessie
Elenbaas, was Erik's wish manager, and she
asked Edgar and me to play evil villains that Erik
would "defeat" in order to save Seattle. The prem-
ise was that Edgar would be the villain, "Dr.
Dark," and I would be his accomplice, "Blackout
Boy." Together we would terrorize the city of Seattle until "Electron Boy" swooped in to save the
day. I rented an elaborate costume and put on
black eyeliner to become Blackout Boy, and Edgar
wore medical scrubs and pushed himself around in
an old wheelchair to become Dr. Dark.

Together, we went around Seattle wreaking
havoc while being chased by Electron Boy. First
we held the Seattle Sounders soccer team hostage
at Qwest Field. Then Electron Boy arrived in a
DeLorean with full police escort to free the cap-
tured soccer team with his lightening rod. Once
the team was safe, a video appeared on the stadi-
um's Jumbotron telling Erik that Edgar and I
were now at the Puget Sound Energy Building,

*Jake Anderson and Edgar Hansen*
*(Photo by Jessie Elenbaas)*

*Jake Anderson (Photo by Scott Harder)*

threatening to make the entire city go dark. Erik arrived and stopped us again, this time keeping the city of Seattle from blacking out. Our final stop was the Space Needle, where Edgar and I had trapped civilians on the observation deck. When we arrived at the Space Needle, Jessie said to me, "This is the most important part. Erik has a lightning rod. If he hits you with his rod, you have to freeze." So when Erik arrived at the Space Needle, he ran up to me and started beating me over the head with his lightening rod, which resembled a Darth Vader lightsaber. Everyone got a good laugh because I had to "freeze" while Erik kept smacking me on the head. After Erik defeated me, he made us apologize for all the atrocities we had done to the city.

*Erik Martin and Jake Anderson*
*(Photo by Scott Harder)*

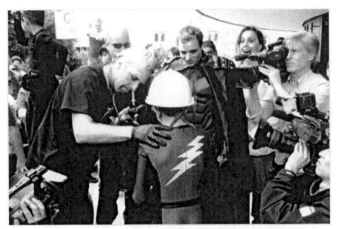

*(From left) Edgar Hansen, Erik Martin, Jake Anderson*
*(Photo by Scott Harder)*

I did one more Make-A-Wish event, and it was at the Hard Rock Cafe in Seattle. It was the same weekend as my dad's funeral, and I was driving home with Jenna when I received a call from Jessie. She told me that a thirteen year-old boy named Simone had flown all the way from Italy to fulfill his wish of becoming a rock star. Simone was going to play guitar with former Guns N' Roses bassist, Duff McKagan, and the local band, *Rewind*. Jessie invited me to join them on stage for their performance. I was coming off an exhausting weekend, but I knew this was too good to pass up. I arrived at the Hard Rock and they brought me on stage to play guitar for the last song, which was Nirvana's *Smells Like Teen Spirit.* Playing a Nirvana song on the same stage where they once performed was probably my wish, too.

As far as getting recognized from the show, the money I've earned, and the incredible things I've been able to do, nothing compares to what it feels like to give back to the community. It's the best part of being a "reality star," and it's definitely the most rewarding. I'll never be able to repay the Anacortes community for what they did for my dad, but Jenna and I will try for the rest of our lives.

# Relapse

*"But they that wait upon the Lord shall renew their strength; they shall mount up with wings as eagles; they shall run, and not be weary; and they shall walk, and not faint."* – Isaiah 40:31

My biggest fear in writing this book is that it would lead to another relapse. Not because I miss drugs or alcohol, but because people who write success stories about how they've been "cured" of their addictions tend to drink and die. It's sacrilegious to promote drug and alcohol treatment programs, which is why I've been nervous to even use words like *support program* in this book. It goes against the tradition of these programs to talk about them in press, radio, or film. They are programs of attraction rather than promotion. Throughout this book I've been careful not to mention what specific program I'm in or what I'm doing to stay sober. It's not because I think writing about support programs is a curse, it's just the thought of relapsing scares the shit out of me.

When I wonder if I'll have the courage to stay sober for the rest of my life, I remember back to the day I finally gave up my addiction. It was July 20th, 2009, and I was doing maintenance work on the *Northwestern* at the Pacific Fishermen Shipyard. I had just heard the replay of an interview in which Sig, Johnathan Hillstrand, and Keith Colburn said I was one of the most loyal and hardworking deckhands they had ever seen. They said I was the type of guy they wanted to have working on their boats. When I heard that, I thought, "How can they say that? That's not me. I'm no good. I'm nobody." Here were people that I looked up to saying great things about me, and I felt like they were lying. I felt like a fraud. Hearing that interview and feeling as bad as I did, it made me want to be a better person. But I wanted to be a better person for *myself*, and not for any other reason. That's when I started to change. I didn't straighten up my life to improve my career, or because I wanted to keep my girlfriend or make my family proud. It was none of those reasons. I did it because I was selfish, and that's the only way I've managed to stay sober. From that day forward I changed everything I did. It was almost like I started living my life backwards. I used to drink because of myself, and now I *didn't* drink because of myself. I changed everything–it was that simple. And I've been sober since July 20$^{th}$, 2009.

I don't regret being an alcoholic and an addict. If I was neither of those things, then I wouldn't have grown and matured to the point where I could deal with situations like losing my dad and my sister. I would have been consumed by these losses and I might not have come back. If I didn't learn the discipline taught through my support program, then I would have made a stupid decision that hurt myself or somebody else. There could have been a million different things that happened and I still think about the "what ifs" today.

As I write this, I still have to live day by day and sometimes hour by hour. That's how I remain. I run through possible scenarios in my head. What if this happened, would I use? Or if that happened, would I turn to alcohol? The answer is always no. Every time. Over the past five years I've learned that I have to put my sobriety first, before everything else. Even when my dad was missing, I had to worry about myself first, and my dad and my family second. If I don't take care of myself, then I can't take care of those around me. It's selfish, but it's the only way an addict can survive.

I remember praying to God when I was living on the streets for a way out of the Hell I was in. He taught me to embrace life and to go through the journey being the strongest man I can be. He also taught me to never forget who I am or where I came from. When I go back to Anacortes, it hits me like a brick wall. I remember who I was, what I did, and how far I've come. I live every day to distance myself from the pain I used to feel there. For me, the fear of relapsing will always be present, but I'm learning to live in less fear.